DYSPRAXIA
IN THE
EARLY YEARS

DYSPRAXIA
IN THE
EARLY YEARS

Identifying and Supporting Children with Movement Difficulties

CHRISTINE MACINTYRE

David Fulton Publishers
London

David Fulton Publishers Ltd
Ormond House, 26–27 Boswell Street, London WC1N 3JZ

www.fultonpublishers.co.uk

First published in Great Britain by David Fulton Publishers 2000
Reprinted 2000, 2001

Note: The right of Christine Macintyre to be identified as the author of this work
has been asserted by her in accordance with the Copyright, Designs and Patents
Act 1988.

Copyright © Christine Macintyre 2000

British Library Cataloguing in Publication Data
A catalogue record for this book is available from the British Library

ISBN 1–85346–677–8

371.91672/

Typeset by Textype Typesetters, Cambridge
Printed in Great Britain by The Cromwell Press Ltd, Trowbridge, Wilts.

Contents

Acknowledgements

There are many people who have contributed to this book and I would like to thank them all. First, a huge thank you to all the teachers and nursery nurses who participated in the research, who allowed me to observe, record and film in their schools, and who patiently answered many questions and asked even more!

Thank you too, to all the parents who shared their experiences of living with dyspraxia, their frustrations when things were difficult and their joys when progress was made.

And of course the children. They were fascinating and responsive and they need a special mention, and a very sincere thank you for trying the activities, and letting me know what they thought!

Thank you too, to the people who prepared the text. Shauna Quinton who produced the text and proofread patiently and professionally. Aileen Robertson for the helpful graphics and Andrew Mayle, who filmed the children then made stills from the film.

Everyone gave much time and expertise to pulling the results of this research together. They thought that a text outlining all our findings would interest others who were anxious to help children with dyspraxia but didn't quite know how. So, here it is and I hope it does!

Foreword

In this book, Dr Christine Macintyre points out that all young children who are not moving well can be helped. However, some movement difficulties, even though they are significant, are hard to identify. The book explains how to spot and analyse different movement difficulties, even those which may not be immediately obvious to the ordinary observer, and how to help the children who are affected by them.

Motor development is too important, in itself and because it can affect other aspects of a child's development, to be left to chance. Furthermore, we cannot assume that children who have motor difficulties when they are very young will grow out of them. To teachers and parents who want to know how to help young children who do not move well, this book not only gives practical suggestions but also points out that 'helping means understanding'. It offers understanding by explaining in a readable way a field which is complex and of course has its own specialist terms. The book, together with its useful pictures which show the difficulties and the implications of e.g. poor muscle tone, comes from Dr Macintyre's most recent research. During that research she spent time working with teachers who had children in their classes who had been described as 'clumsy' and with parents who, having worried privately on their own, were strangely relieved to discover that many others were worried about their children's movement development too. They were glad to hear about a study by The Dyspraxia Trust which reported that 8–10 per cent of children have difficulty in moving well. Above all, Dr Macintyre spent time understanding and working with the children themselves.

I believe that this is a useful book and that many nursery and infant teachers and many parents will feel encouraged when they read it.

Margot Cameron-Jones
Professor of Teacher Education
The University of Edinburgh

Introduction

This text aims to enable all those who are closely involved with the development and education of young children to do three things. Firstly, to be able to identify movement difficulties in young children; secondly, to understand these specific difficulties and the wider implications for coping at home and at school; and thirdly to know what can be done to help at home and in the nursery and infant classrooms.

The text is based on four years of research which involved many parents, teachers, nursery nurses, student teachers and, most importantly of course, the children themselves; and their accounts and ideas and comments form the basis of this book.

The book tackles the questions all of these people asked about the children in their care, e.g. we know there is something wrong but what and why, and what can we do? It suggests ways of observing the children, identifying and understanding their movement difficulties and ways of helping them to cope.

It gives a lively account of the children themselves. Their photos are stills from a video taken when the children were playing out of doors on an ordinary nursery day. This is to try to capture a movement picture and to introduce you to Ellen, Tom, Ben, Ian, Alys, Jake and Derek, real children who may very well be like your own!

This is a positive book. It can honestly say, 'Yes, these children have difficulties and some of them are severe. But if we all understand and take appropriate steps, these children can be helped.'

This is why the main emphasis is on analysing movement patterns – understanding what is and what ought to be. Movement difficulties can be identified early, indeed they may be one of the first signs that help is required. For if identification is early, help, intervention, remediation, call it what you will, can be early too. And all the latest research, e.g. Kirby (1999), McMillan and Leslie

(1998), is claiming that that is the best way forward. Hopefully early intervention will do as much as possible to help the children become more effective and confident movers and thus prevent the emergence of other related difficulties – a very important thing to try to do.

But what is involved in helping? It is not easy. It means understanding the problems these children have, observing then analysing their movement patterns, recognising the wider implications which may accompany movement difficulties, getting to grips with programmes of activities which will help the children cope more easily and above all staying positive and enthusiastic so that the children themselves can recognise and appreciate the progress they have made. This book tries to provide insights and guidance to encourage all those who aim to maximise their children's learning in this kind of way.

And the biggest achievement for all of us will be when our children say,

'Look at us, we can do it too!'

Photo 1 Isn't this fun?

Please note that the names of all the people in the book have been changed to protect their identity. For the same reason the faces in some of the photographs have been blurred.

CHAPTER 1

Young children and movement

By the time they are five – or six or seven – most children have made tremendous strides in their motor development. They can run and jump and climb and swing and many like to challenge themselves further by adding bicycles or roller blades, even skis! Some love to dance and can learn complex step patterns. These activities require quite a sophisticated sense of rhythm, balance and coordination but give great enjoyment and satisfaction. Acquiring these skills also allows the children to join in group activities and so they learn the social skills of playing together, e.g. turn-taking and sharing and following someone else's lead. They learn to follow the 'rules' in a game and so begin to empathise with children who win and those that lose. All of this is part of the rough and tumble of growing up.

But some do not develop the movement skills which allow these things to happen. For them, coping with everyday activities is challenging enough, even overwhelmingly difficult. And these can be bright children with no apparent neurological disorder. So what is wrong? Why should some children be limited in this way? Why can they not do the things other children enjoy? And what will the effect on their confidence and self-esteem be?

These children must be helped at a very early age for all of the reasons above, because children learning motor skills 'out-of-step' with their chronological age may find it much harder and because

> it is widely accepted that the development of controlled movement has a part to play in the development of thinking and understanding. Children need to experience movement in order to learn about themselves, their relationship to the environment and the interaction of the two. (French and Lee 1994)

So the ability to move well is important in its own right and because it permeates into other facets of the children's development, e.g. learning about themselves and how to cope in a changing, more demanding world.

It can be understood then that movement difficulties can be complex and long-lasting, even with help. Furthermore, children have different blends of long-lasting difficulties and different levels of disability and this can make accurate diagnosis quite tricky. However, activities to help can be fun as well as being effective, and this should be the aim of any remedial programme. Children without difficulties can join in too. No-one need feel different. In this way all the children can look forward to movement lessons, especially if difficulties are dealt with in a calm, 'let's practise' kind of way and the children are helped to reflect on the progress they have made.

An important benefit of early intervention is that very young children tend to be engrossed in their own activities and so are less likely to compare their own performance negatively with others more skilled in this motor field. Hopefully with appropriate and timely help, their difficulties can be alleviated before others become aware of them and before they themselves become distressed and reluctant to try. Certainly Caan (1998) has claimed that 'clumsiness is not an indelible label' and Portwood (1998) that the earlier the intervention, the greater the chance of success.

Education in nurseries and primaries today has a large practical component. 'Handling materials', 'investigating', 'problem-solving' – these kinds of learning experiences permeate the curriculum. Once more, emphasis is being placed on handwriting skills (Ripley *et al.* 1997) so children who find moving difficult may be unable to function as well as their intellectual capacity should allow. For how can children with poor muscle control in their upper limbs learn to write? Digue and Kettles (1996) agree that motor dysfunction can confuse adults into thinking that children are of a lower ability than is the case.

Before we begin to consider movement difficulties, it is perhaps a good idea to look briefly at what is involved in moving well, because moving efficiently and effectively in different environments tends to be taken for granted with few people really appreciating the complex interplay of intellectual and motor abilities which occurs.

For moving well means,

- controlling the body as it moves
- coordinating different body parts so that movement is smooth
- gauging the correct amount of strength and speed
- understanding directionality
- being able to manipulate objects
- appreciating the rhythm of movements to aid repetition
- making safety decisions about when to move and where to move, and
- being able to stay still!

A complex achievement, is it not?

Photo 2 Phew!

When does it all begin?

Of course children are moving long before they are born but it's difficult to know what kind of learning is happening then! But what we do know is that from their very earliest post-natal days, children are constantly learning to move and moving to learn, and this learning means that all aspects of development change.

Dividing development up under the headings motor, intellectual, social and emotional is really a ploy to make the study of development manageable, for it is a huge topic covering many fields. Each aspect has its own specialist body of knowledge, but of course children don't develop in discrete pathways – development in one area affects all of the others, some more, some less (see Figure 1.1).

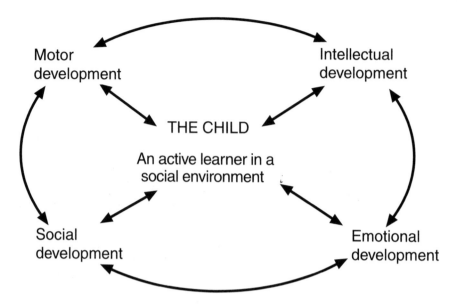

Figure 1.1 The interplay of different aspects of development

Two examples will try to show this interdependency.

Example 1 Reaching and grasping

Picture Ellen, a baby of four months or so lying in her cot with a mobile suspended above her. She is fascinated by the bright colours of the toy and follows it with her eyes as it swings. She reacts by moving her arms and legs in a random uncoordinated way and by chance a hand strikes the mobile. This happens again and again and gradually Ellen comes to realise that she has caused the toy to move. She practises this until she can reach more accurately. At the same time her crooning noises attract Mum who is delighted with Ellen's progress and she gives her daughter a hug.

What has Ellen learned so far? Well, in reaching out she has learned that her hand could make things happen, about how far away the mobile was, what direction her stretch needed to have and where her own body finished and the outside object began. These are elementary kinesthetic learnings – body awareness, spatial awareness, directionality and body boundary, which are primarily concerned with motor learning but a great deal of intellectual gain has been made as well. For Ellen has been learning elementary tracking, i.e. following an object along a pathway, a skill she will develop in reading later on. She has also been learning what happens to an object when it is touched, a very early lesson in cause and effect!

Then her Mum's reaction helped her emotional development. She was secure in the knowledge that she had pleased, and the hug reinforced the idea that it was good for her to try again. And so moving had also helped communication, an aspect of social development.

Now Ellen wants to have the toy. At first her striking actions are too hard and the toy swings out of reach, but gradually she learns how much strength to use and as the toy strikes her palm, she begins to time and refine the grasping action. Now she has it, but can't let go! Letting go is a much more sophisticated action which needs lots of practice, but babies are motivated – they are skill hungry and she will persevere.

Grasping the toy is a significant achievement for Ellen and again this brings forth praise from her parents who are anxiously noting and applauding her progress in achieving her motor milestones. Moreover, she realises that she can move her arm and hand independently; she doesn't require a whole body movement to accomplish her task. This is an important step towards using segmented, precise movements rather than whole body movements which are cumbersome and inefficient.

She enjoys doing things well and as a result her confidence rises. Her emotional development has been strengthened again. And certainly others will come to admire her and so she learns to enjoy being the centre of attention. Perhaps she even learns how to control her audience by crying when they move away! Intellectual? Social? Emotional? Perhaps all of them, and all coming from a movement base!

Example 2 Crawling

Many of the parents in the research said that their children had not crawled. Ben's Dad, James, explained, 'At the time, we didn't think not crawling was significant, in fact we thought Ben had been quite smart and missed a stage out, but when we met other people and chatted about Ben's difficulties, they invariably asked, "Did he crawl?"' And so James wanted to find why crawling was so important and what vital learning the children who didn't crawl had missed.

First, crawling is a form of locomotion or travelling and being able to crawl means that the environment is waiting to be explored and the child is in charge of making decisions about when to move, where to go, how fast to travel and what to explore. And so the child has a measure of independence, probably for the first time.

Some children of course, can move around by rolling over and over, but learning to crawl has other benefits. First, the children who crawl take up a prone kneeling position and this helps strengthen the muscles around the shoulders and hips. They will be a little unsteady and fine adjustments are needed to hold the position. This all helps body awareness and the developing sense of balance. Then, as one arm is raised to stretch out, balance has to be held on three points, and more subtle adjustments have to be made. The extended arm investigates direction and distance, and these are important learning experiences for understanding positions in space.

The actual crawling action itself is a complex sequence of movements where the arms and legs work in opposition. This patterning and coordination seem to help other forms of sequential activities, e.g. ordering which is important in learning to count and understanding the logic of 'beginning, middle and end' in storytelling. And so a vast amount of motor and intellectual learning has been acquired by children who have learned to crawl.

But what about the social and emotional aspects of development? Well, a great deal of confidence is gained from being independent, provided of course that there aren't too many unsupervised bumps, and socially the children are able to move to join in 'games' with others, perhaps even initiating a chasing game! And even very basic games have social parameters, e.g. turn-taking and looking out for others, and intellectual demands, e.g. empathising with the others, possibly non-speaking 'players', appreciating what they do, then planning an appropriate movement response.

And so, if children don't do these kinds of activities, they are missing valuable learning opportunities in all aspects of their development. And if they don't attempt them at the 'right' time – what some authors, e.g. Child (1986), claim as 'the critical learning time' – they may be disinclined to try later. He is suggesting that the acquisition of the skills is age-related. However, there may also be psychological reasons why activities can be avoided. An adult learning to ski may well be put off by the five year old skimming past! When adults and children without difficulties do try, however, they 'seem minimally affected by deprivation and improve rapidly with practice and training'. In making this claim Digue and Kettles 1996 are taking a different standpoint to Child. However they both agree that those with problems have a much more difficult time.

If you look back at Figure 1.1 now, you will see that at the centre is 'the active child in a social environment'. These words were chosen to remind us that each child is a lively young person who will interact with his or her environment in a different way. Children are not passive recipients of other people's learning. They actively seek out experiences which will help them to make sense of their world. From the start, they are problem-solvers who test out hypotheses, or ideas about how things might work, and they store their solutions in their memories. In this way they build a repertoire of skills, hopefully in a well-supervised environment.

Each child will react in different ways due to their individual personality characteristics. Some children appear fearless and have to be watched every moment they are awake. They need 'angels watching over them', while others ponder, seemingly weighing up the likely consequences of what they might do. Individual personality characteristics, such as resilience or vulnerability, influence how well the children are able to overcome difficulties. Vulnerable children can be devastated by happenings which the resilient ones manage to shrug off, apparently unconcerned and ready to overcome any obstacle which gets in their way. Furthermore, the children will be influenced by their home environment; perhaps in the value they place on different kinds of activities – even on wanting to learn!

It might be easier if all children were the same and we could anticipate how they would react and progress, but this doesn't happen. Those who try to help them therefore have to decentre, i.e. put themselves in the children's place and try to gauge the kinds of learning experiences which will be of greatest benefit for each child.

CHAPTER 2

Identifying children with movement difficulties

Let's think now about children we know who don't cope very well with the activities of daily living so that we can try to identify what is amiss. Do they perhaps

- move in an ungainly, uncoordinated way?
- appear reluctant to try new activities?
- crash into things?
- get tired and irritable easily?
- not hear when asked to do something?
- begin a job then forget what comes next?
- have no sense of time or urgency?
- find it difficult to concentrate?
- have difficulty speaking clearly?
- find it difficult to track a moving object?

And do they find it difficult, even impossible to

- manage fiddly things like buttons?
- let someone near them for a hug?
- join in games especially if there are 'rules?'
- make two hands work together?
- stand still and wait?

Some children with movement difficulties have several of these symptoms, others just one or two – and the degree of difficulty varies as well. This first level of diagnosis is useful because the effects need careful consideration. Why, for example, are the children tetchy and irritable? Is it because they realise that other people are tired of them dropping things? Or is it because they have to concentrate so hard to work out what to do next, or because no one will let them play? This kind of reflection allows carers to empathise with the children and understand their perspective, for these children don't intend or want to cause the upsets which occur so often in their day.

Parents tell

When Ian's Mum, Lynn, described her feelings in coming to realise that Ian had difficulty coordinating his movements and generally keeping up with his friends, she explained, 'I couldn't think what was wrong. He smiled and reacted to us just as we had expected, but when he moved he stayed at the baby stage, taking a long time to get better at doing things. When he pulled himself up to standing at the couch, he had to hold on very hard to try to steady himself; we noticed that although he wanted a biscuit, he couldn't stretch out to get it. To do that he had to plonk down first and often he'd fall backwards, hitting his head and then he'd howl! This went on for a very long time. I think he'd be 20 months before he could coordinate actions like that. Even then, if he dropped his biscuit he couldn't bend down to retrieve it. I thought he was the only one like this and I wondered what had caused the problem. I thought I must have done something wrong, maybe not letting him do things by himself enough, or not giving him vitamins to strengthen his bones.'

In recalling these early experiences, Lynn had raised some important points which were confusing other parents and causing them unnecessary anguish.

First, the number of children. The parents were surprised, and in a strange way 'kind of relieved', to hear that their child was not the only one, in fact that 8–10 per cent of all children have some degree of difficulty in moving well (Dyspraxia Trust 1991). This is a significant number. Teachers and nursery nurses need to know the figures too, for it indicates that there are likely to be two or three such children in every class. The Trust also claims that boys are affected more than girls, in a ratio of 4:1, although girls, when they are affected, are usually more severely disabled.

Realising this, the parents felt less isolated and felt more confident in sharing their worries with the teachers who they considered would understand, because it was very likely that there would be other children needing the same kind of help. They also knew that their children were entitled to have their difficulties recognised and helped.

In the research which prompted this book, the teachers and nursery nurses in school claimed that four or even five out of each group of 33 children had movement difficulties. This was slightly higher than the norm. Perhaps being involved in new research biased the observers or perhaps, and this is more likely given the care and written criteria which led the research, there are more children needing help out there than was previously identified. Of course any incidence figure can be significantly affected by the content of the assessment and the conditions under which it is applied, even the observational skill or the cultural expectations of the designers of the assessments themselves.

Another possible influence on any statistic lies in the parents' right not to have their children assessed. They may fear labelling or mistakenly believe that scores are going to be bandied about. If these parents should have children with movement problems and withdraw their children from any assessment, then the figures are going to be skewed.

In this research, only two sets of parents were not willing for their children to be assessed. The researchers explained that the children would not be aware of assessments being made, that all recording was confidential and that the point of the research was to help the children, but the parents were against assessment of any kind and this was respected.

Other statistics highlight the importance of recognising and helping, sadly not curing dyspraxia. Stephenson and Fairgrieve (1996) found that 23:31 children with developmental coordination disorder had specific learning difficulties necessitating learning support, half of that number needing help with reading, writing and spelling. Kirby (1999) claims that, 'it is very difficult to find the "pure" child'. She explains that symptoms may well overlap with Asperger's disorder (language/ communication difficulties), with dyslexia (reading difficulties) and ADHD (attention deficit and hyperactivity disorder).

The causes of developmental dyspraxia

The causes of developmental dyspraxia in children have not been clearly identified. Many researchers are trying to do this, but it appears that just as there are several forms of dyspraxia, there are several causes. The difficulty in identifying 'triggers' according to Lehmkuyl (1984) is that these children have no 'obvious physical or neurological abnormality to explain their difficulties, and typically manifest a more diverse set of symptoms than do children with organic brain damage'.

A high proportion of children with movement difficulties, however, do have immature neurone development as a consequence of low birth weight or other perinatal stresses such as viral infections or deprivation of oxygen at birth. Another popular theory is that the 'complex interconnections in the motor cortex have somehow become mixed up, causing information to be processed in a haphazard way' (Digue and Kettles 1996).

If this is the case, it explains why information which should go to specific body parts (e.g. in crawling to one leg and arm) is unfiltered, sending 'moving messages' simultaneously to all four limbs, hence the difficulty in deciding which goes first and coordinating the action. For this reason too, the running child may have the arms raised inappropriately and any one arm action such as throwing may have complementary movement on the other side of the body, although all this does is hamper the movement by preventing the body turn which would give power to the throw.

Carlson *et al.* (1988), studying the development of the nervous system, now consider that faulty neural regression may lead to the difficulties that children with dyspraxia suffer. If the developing system does not rid itself of unwanted neurons and neural networks in the brain, they suggest that this overabundance may lead to 'faulty processing of perceptual information, speech difficulties, a high level of distractibility, hyperactivity and tactile over-sensitivity'. (For a fuller discussion of causes, see Digue and Kettles 1996.)

The parents also confided that in the first instance, admitting their child's difficulty had not been easy, but when they discovered that they were not alone and that steps were being taken to help they were 'still worried but just so relieved to understand and to know that other children were just the same'.

Another critical question raised by several parents was, 'How early can children's difficulties be recognised?' and to answer this, Ann, the mother of a seven year old, Derek, spoke with Susan, his nursery teacher.

Ann: Derek is my second child, and I now have a little girl so I have other children to help me make judgments about his progress. Right from the start I thought he was a little floppy, but you are just so thankful that all the right bits are there that it's easier to dismiss any suspicions that make you uneasy. However by four or five months he wasn't playing with his hands as the others did, nor was he stretching out to try to grip things. I was beginning to be really worried but the doctor obviously thought I was just an over-anxious mum, and anyway what can one do at that age? At a year he was not attempting to crawl – in fact he never did crawl – he simply sat on his bottom till he was 18 months then he walked straight across the floor.

This has been typical. He waits to make sure he is safe before he attempts anything new – he takes time to think through the possibilities of getting hurt; he is very deliberate in his actions. He walked a little late, but not really late enough to worry us – he was about 22 months if I remember, but he always had his toes turned in, and that meant he was always tripping over his feet and falling. When he tried to run he had the strangest gait. He waddled, not lifting his feet far off the ground, and seemed to swing his leg round rather than taking it straight through. Maybe that was because his toes were turned in. He seemed to swing his leg from the hip rather than bending his knee. He didn't have a more normal pattern till he was five. We were so relieved he had achieved that before he went to big school, for we thought the other children might laugh at him.

Susan: Tell me about the things he liked to do and some he didn't.

Photos 3 & 4 Derek

Ann: At a year he was already interested in books, loving the pictures and the stories, and at 20 months he had quite a vocabulary – he had no language delay. But at Nursery he never painted, never played with Lego in the usual building way. He would line the bricks up but never join them up and that was the first indication that he couldn't use two hands together. His fingers still lacked strength and he had obvious coordination difficulties. He couldn't draw a cross and his colouring-in was very immature. Nor could he fit the pieces of a jigsaw together although he could recognise where they should go. Of course he wouldn't be persuaded to try these things so he had never had any practice.

Susan: How did he get on with the other children?

Ann: Not very well. He always played solitary, usually imaginary games. He had a yo-yo which he treated as a dog – this was his 'best friend' and of course the other children didn't understand. When he did ask other children to play, the game always ended in tears. 'They are spoiling my game' he would cry, because he had a clear notion of what the game was to be about and he couldn't bear it to be changed. And he wouldn't or couldn't play when other children were in charge of a game. He didn't seem to be able to grasp what they were trying to do. So he was happier playing alone.

Susan: How does he cope at home?

Ann: He has a number of real difficulties. One is being a messy eater. He finds using a knife and fork incredibly difficult – and as he is seven now that's becoming ever more of a problem. If he is asked out, other parents don't expect him to use his fingers to break up his food. For his own birthday we had a picnic party when we had finger food on the beach. This was to avoid the other children seeing how difficult eating at table is. However, avoiding the problems like this doesn't help in the long run. I think this is hindering him socially. He doesn't get asked to many parties now and in some ways that's easier, although it's heartbreaking as well. Sometimes I think I worry more than him.

Susan: What about other difficulties at home? Can he dress himself?

Ann: I always have put his things out in order and he has a chart for the wall with numbers on each garment. My little girl has dolls in various states of undress and that has been quite helpful as he will tell Lucy, that's my daughter, how the clothes should go on. And so he has got better at dressing himself. But he can't tie shoelaces and the school tie is a nightmare. On PE days he has permission to go to school in trainers but he doesn't like to be different, he doesn't want to admit he can't manage. It's never simple!

Susan: Have you ever tried to get any professional help?

Ann: Oh yes, but because Derek looked strong and could chat to the doctor quite confidently, I was told I was a fussy mother and he would soon manage fine. The doctor asked him to walk around the room and he could do this with no trouble. He also watched him getting up and sitting down – again Derek could do it. Of course he was concentrating hard as he did this and these movements didn't involve the two hands working together, so it wasn't a real assessment, not very satisfactory at all.

And when he went to school we discovered he had another problem. As he had always liked picture books and stories and made up lots of imaginative stories himself, I thought reading would be easy. But no, he had great difficulty, and that's when the school backed my pleas for help. The thing was that they waited until he had other problems, and you can imagine what that did for his confidence. They did give him help in the form of learning support – but being taken out the class for that labels the child as a slow learner. At this stage I insisted on IQ testing, and we found that he had a verbal IQ of 140 but a performance IQ of 98. These results gave us access to physiotherapy and once the problem had been identified, the teachers were really anxious to help, although sometimes I felt they were unsure of the best way.

Ann raised many interesting points in that interview, particularly the discrepancy in the different levels of Derek's IQ, the negative effect of incorrect labelling, the enduring nature of movement difficulties, the possible link with reading difficulties and above all perhaps, the social sadnesses that arise from not being able to cope with all of the activities that are an important part of childhood. She brought out very clearly the psychological difficulties for parents in insisting that their child has a problem when the experts say not, and when they so want to believe them. She also considered that schools needed extra information about children with movement difficulties.

Interestingly, Ann explained that when she did have help, the physiotherapist called Derek's difficulties 'dyspraxia'. While this was confusing, she was relieved that he had a recognised condition which showed he was not alone!

Other parents reinforced the points that Ann made, particularly in relation to their children

- never having crawled
- reaching their motor milestones late
- finding interacting with their peer group difficult
- preferring the company of younger children
- not having the same interests as other children
- being left out, never being chosen
- finding using two hands together very difficult
- never crossing the midline, changing hands instead.

They also agreed that they had suspected something was amiss in their child's first year and several claimed that requests for help had been rebuffed. Possibly this was because children with movement difficulties look no different from other children and while no-one would wish otherwise, this causes the children to be denied the sympathy and understanding that they require, either in the level of expectation of movement tasks or in the time they need to complete them. Sugden and Keoch (1991) explain that these children have 'a hidden handicap'.

On reflection, parents and teachers realised that before the children's difficulties were explained, they might have blamed their children for being clumsy or late or forgetful or 'for never ever being able to hurry up!'. They knew that this kind of reaction only made things worse, but 'sometimes it's hard to remember, and then all the frustration spills out'.

Movement difficulties occur across the whole spectrum of intelligence. They are pervasive and disabling, but children *can* be helped. And perhaps when they become adults, life will be easier, because then they can choose the things they would like to do.

You will have noticed that the term 'dyspraxia' has been used interchangeably with movement difficulties and developmental coordination disorder has also been mentioned, and so now is a good time to consider the terminologies which are being applied by different groups of professionals.

Movement difficulties or dyspraxia: what's in a name?

There have been several descriptors given to the condition I've called 'movement difficulties' as different groups of professionals have struggled to find a term which accurately and comprehensively describes their view of the difficulties children display. Some terms have stayed in vogue for a time and then been discarded, because as more is understood, they have become inadequate! It is interesting to discover why other titles have sprung up in their place, because the reasoning behind the choice tells something of the developing understanding of the complexities of the condition.

Children with movement difficulties used to be called 'clumsy'. This was certainly an easy-to-understand, commonly used term. It conjured up a picture of a lovable, harum-scarum lad who fell over his own feet but who got up smiling! However the word 'clumsy' somehow implied blame. It suggested that if the children just went a little slower or took more care, all would be well. Sadly this is not the case. Furthermore, these children, deep down, were not smiling even if smiling was a strategy for survival. They were much more likely to be hurt and disillusioned and wary of trying again.

And so this term was supplanted by 'minimal motor impairment' and this seemed to fit the bill for some time until it was realised that some people weren't sure what it meant. Was 'motor', for example, the same as 'movement' and what level of impairment was 'minimal'? Moreover, the descriptor 'impairment' didn't really suggest that progress could be made, and this is incorrect and so a more accurate name had to be found.

One was 'Developmental Coordination Disorder' or 'DCD' and that is a useful descriptor in that it indicates that coordination is at the root of the children's difficulties and this is critically important. However the adjective 'developmental' suggests to me that the children will 'grow out of it', that is that maturation alone will overcome any difficulties. This suggestion is misleading in my view, because without help, the children with movement difficulties are not at all likely to reach their full potential. Despite this and despite the long name however, this descriptor remains a popular choice. It embraces the concept that the children thus described will have a lower performance ability than could be expected from their chronological age and their other abilities, even though this is not apparent from the title!

Those who favour the term 'DCD' explain that it differentiates between children with coordination difficulties and those who have dyspraxia, which when used accurately means that children have motor planning difficulties *and* perceptual problems (Kirby 1999). Not all children with movement difficulties, however, have this added burden.

One of the most recent attempts to find a solution is the title 'motor-based learning difficulties' and this is pleasing in that it shows that movement difficulties may exacerbate other conditions such as poor behaviour due to frustration, or link with other difficulties such as dyslexia. My fear, however, is that the stress will then be placed on helping these other things rather than tackling the movement difficulties themselves. This is based on many years of finding that other problem areas, e.g. reading and mathematics, take priority, even although movement difficulties which are apparent much earlier are ignored. This is what happened to Derek. Waiting until children fail is a poor educational strategy in my view.

The most widely used term today seems to be 'dyspraxia' (dys = faulty and praxis = the ability to use the body as a skilled tool). The difficulty here is that different groups of professionals use it as a global term to describe their own sets of criteria, while others consider that the term should only be used if the children have been scored on accredited tests. This variety of use can be confusing. Having said that, some parents have told me that they were relieved to have the diagnosis, 'dyspraxia'. Possibly this was because the title could justify their appeals for help, or perhaps, knowing that children with dyslexia and dysgraphia were being helped in school, they considered that teachers would understand the needs of children with dyspraxia.

The 'new labels' which abound in schools today make one wonder about the accuracy of diagnosis. Are the labels being applied too liberally? Is every child who is a little slow to read, dyslexic? Certainly there are criteria to guide in the confirmation of dyspraxia, and these are listed below, but there is no benchmark, no cut off point which distinguishes the child with dyspraxia from another (Kirby 1999). Perhaps the dyspraxic child meets more of the criteria, but at what level of difficulty?

The five criteria from The Diagnostic and Statistical Manual of the American Psychiatric Association are:

1. There is a marked impairment in the development of motor coordination.
2. The impairment significantly interferes with academic performance or the activities of daily living.
3. The coordination difficulties are not due to medical conditions such as cerebral palsy, hemiplegia or muscular dystrophy.
4. It is not a pervasive developmental disorder.
5. If motor delay is evident, the motor difficulties are in excess of those usually associated with it.

My own preference rests with the term 'movement difficulties' used as an umbrella term to cover all aspects of learning to move, i.e. accurately interpreting signals from the environment (perceiving), knowing what to do (planning/organising), as well as carrying out the movement (doing or executing), because all of these work together to make movement effective and efficient. If one component is faulty then the others suffer too.

In addition this term can be legitimately applied to those children who do not have the severe perceptual difficulties which are part of true dyspraxia. I also feel that this term is acceptable to teachers and nursery nurses in the classroom who need to help children with a whole spectrum of difficulties. In the research which prompted this book, most teachers were wary of 'giving children labels which make them feel different, especially in the first years at school when progress can be significant'. When they were asked why, given that labels such as 'dyspraxic' were meant to be helpful as they showed that the children had a recognised problem which was not their fault, the teachers and parents had several things to say:

Labels first of all say there is something wrong, and these children are too young. Surely nothing is fixed at this age, and surely careful teaching is enough?

Once there is a label, parents and most people who don't understand think the children are going to have all of the difficulties of dyspraxia and it may be just one or two, so panic sets in where there's no need.

I like all my children to know that everyone is different; we all have talents and difficulties. What about the ones who can't sing? If we have labels, then we need one for them and another for children who have eczema. Where does it stop?

But others disagreed:

It's alright provided people know what dyspraxia means and that it's not something catching. One person asked me if the children needed injections!

It's much better to have any condition identified, to have everything out in the open. Then people learn about how teachers have to cope with all sorts of problems. It's when nobody mentions it, that sinister ideas spread.

It's the only way to get proper help, because the classroom can only cope up to a point. We don't have the resources to help, much as we'd like to. We need physiotherapy input. That's essential. And the only way to get it, is to say that the children definitely have dyspraxia.

Unfortunately, access to physiotherapy/occupational therapy is not always easy and in most cases, especially with children who are mildly, even moderately affected, teachers just have to cope. And as more research unfolds and the complexities become known, coping effectively calls for a greater depth of knowledge and understanding than ever before.

Interestingly a recent Canadian conference was entitled, 'Children and Clumsiness: A Disability in Search of a Title'.

I rest my case!

Nursery teachers tell

Let's listen now to informal observations made by just one nursery teacher describing children who were in their second year at nursery. Let's find the kinds of things which she had idenitfied as causing concern. She recognised that these children had movement difficulties and was anxious that they obtained help before they had to cope with the demands of Primary 1.

Photo 5 Tom

It was a lovely sunny day and as she spoke, we were watching the children playing out of doors on large apparatus. The teacher was also able to reflect on other aspects of the children's behaviour in the nursery.

'Here's Tom. He's a harum-scarum child whose clothes are always in a tangle. He's a big, well-built boy for 4½ and he is forever running too fast and crashing into the other children, or the apparatus or me! He doesn't realise his own strength; he just doesn't slow down and he usually has two skinned knees. He won't wait for his turn on the climbing frame; he just barges in and climbs so fiercely that the whole thing shakes. The other children don't complain, possibly because of his size, although to be fair he has never deliberately hurt anyone.

'He can run and climb and jump but with no control and no sense of self-preservation. Everything has to be done with a clatter. Indoors he is very clumsy. He knocks the building towers over, he spills the paint on the floor, he treats the toys roughly and of course, they break. At this moment in time he's realising that some of the children, in fact most of them, don't want him to play. He doesn't know how to cope with this and there have been one or two occasions when he has deliberately provoked children by spoiling their game. This is a very disturbing new trait. In the past he was smiling and readily forgiven, but antagonism is building up.

Photo 6 Ben

'**Ben** is a complete contrast to Tom. He is 4¾ but a smaller, finer build and he has very poor muscle tone. His arms especially are floppy; they just hang, and even when Ben runs he doesn't use his arms in the usual forward–back action which provides momentum; they just dangle by his sides. When he climbs on the frame he will put out his arms to steady himself, but they give little support and certainly give no help in pulling up. When he jumps down he topples over, and whereas most children would instinctively put out their arms to save themselves, Ben falls on to his shoulders or bangs his head. Once he leaves the scaled-down nursery apparatus, this could be very dangerous. When he tries to throw a ball, he puts all his upper-body strength into the action, but the arms just can't follow through; there is no projection and so the throw has no power. This is frustrating for the child and demoralising when the other children laugh. He does kick the ball with reasonable force, but the lack of strength in the top half of his body means that balancing is difficult and this affects the direction of the kick, and the way the ball travels, i.e. not very fast and not very far!

'Indoors, painting is just flopping paint anywhere on the paper and there is no way he can draw a circle or a rainbow because he hasn't the finger control to hold a pencil. When he tries to draw a circle he does the right side with his right hand and then changes the pencil over to his left. It's as if his body was divided into two halves! And when he sits on the carpet at story time, his top begins to sag as if his arms are too heavy and are pulling him down. However, he is a bright, happy child.

I don't think he realises his limitations yet, but how is he going to cope in the primary school when a more imposed timetable of activities means that he can't avoid things he cannot do?

'And here's **Graeme** at last. He's out-of-puff because he is late. His mum says she has never seen a child who takes so long to get ready. Most days she has to dress him because otherwise he'd never get here in time. One day Graeme asked me, "What is valuable time?" Obviously he'd been found guilty of wasting it!

'Mum explains that even if she lays out all his clothes, he can't decide what goes on first. Often he wants to put his vest over his shirt! Even with velcro shoes he can't cope. Her criteria for choosing a primary school is "later starting in the morning and no ties!" In the Nursery it's the same story, Graeme doesn't seem to be able to follow a sequence of instructions. If he is asked to put his painting over to dry and then go for his snack, he'll do the first – or at least he'll wander over in the right direction, but by then he's forgotten all about what he's to do next. We need to watch when he goes to the toilet or he'll spend ages watching the water swirling down the plug. He doesn't seem to have any sense of time at all – "do this and then that" instructions are lost with Graeme; he can't retain the information, so we always tell him one thing at a time or break down any activity into small steps.

'And when he works on a jigsaw he concentrates so hard – he doesn't glance up or talk to anyone; it seems as if he has to shut everything else out. It's the same when he's building in the construction corner. He takes a huge pile of bricks into a corner and faces the wall as if he has to shut out everything else. He gets very tense. What should be playing seems very hard work for this child.

'On the big apparatus outside, he does one action at a time, not very well. Maybe he clambers over a bench, but then he wanders around quite aimlessly almost as if he needs time to plan what to do next. However, when he eventually gets in line for a turn and reaches the frame or the bench, he has to stop and think; he hasn't planned ahead at all. This causes all sorts of jostling problems. He doesn't respond well if you say, 'What would you like to do now?' He just shrugs you off . . . it's difficult to know what to do. In fact he doesn't like anyone getting too close and invading his personal space.

'**Alys** is the little girl holding on fiercely to the nursery nurse. She is now coming outside without tears, but she'd much rather stay indoors playing quietly in the house corner. Outside, she doesn't seem to know what to do, and so the large apparatus has been a real challenge for her. She has great difficulty even walking slowly along the broad side of a low bench, yet when she does manage it, her face lights up and she is so pleased. To persuade her to come outside we put some coloured plastic hoops on the ground and she will pick these up and even put them over her head, but she won't risk anything that requires balancing on one foot, even briefly. She can't hop or skip. She sometimes will take little jumps over a rope on the

Photo 7 Alys

ground, but not voluntarily – she has to be persuaded, and although she will now walk very gently along the broad side of a bench, there's no way she would jump off it. She always has to reach out tentatively for the ground as if it would disappear. We hoped to do some crawling on the grass to see if Alys had that kind of coordination, but she wouldn't try. She gets very nervous when the other children run around; her shoulders are tight and she quickly gets out of the way.

'Perhaps her lack of confidence stems from her poor speech – she has articulation problems – or at least we can't always make out what she is saying. She doesn't have a lot of confidence so we try to understand without getting her to repeat things or ask her not to mumble. However, the other children seem to understand, and that's a big help! Indoors she spends much of her time in the house corner. When she does choose to draw, the figures she makes are tiny, just in one corner of the page. Her colouring-in is usually done with just one colour and she doesn't have any awareness of the lines, however she is coming on. She is making progress.

'Ian is a gentle, quiet child who generally copes quite well, but he does bump into things – in a much less aggressive way than Sam, for he has a much slower pace. However, when he tries to crawl through hoops, just to take one example, his feet always get tangled and the hoops fall over. Putting his arms into coat sleeves is another difficult job – often he just sits on his coat and waits for help. His body awareness is very poor. When we try songs like "Head and shoulders, knees and toes", he watches the others and copies – and of course he is always one step behind. This doesn't seem to worry him for he is always smiling. Thinking about this made me realise that in other activities he is slow to begin although he's always willing to be involved. He seems to need a minute to watch what the others do. Perhaps he's not hearing properly – he does seem to prefer the quieter areas. I'll find out from his mum whether she has noticed this. At home he is the third child and maybe Mum helps him rather a lot. He is rather babyish, but a very lovable boy!'

Talking about Ian raises the question of maturation. Will the children grow naturally out of some of these difficulties without taking steps to improve their performance? Will increased growth and strength and more experience be enough? For those six and seven year olds, adolescents and adults who still have difficulties, the answer seems to be 'no' and adults who spoke with me were quite resentful that nothing had been done to help them. As one explained, 'If I'd had a broken leg, I would have got help – but I was just called clumsy and told to try harder. I've missed out on so many things I would have liked to be able to do!' She intended, even as an adult, to be tested for dyspraxia, because only by having the condition identified would she feel exonerated of any feeling of guilt that she didn't try hard enough!

The danger of leaving children without help is that they will either avoid the movements which are difficult, or if this is not possible they will try to compensate and cover up problem areas. And once poor patterns are entrenched, it is really difficult to make changes. And as the children's awareness of what others can do is growing all the time, we would not want to leave them to make negative comparisons and be disillusioned by their own performance.

Think of children who can't catch a ball because they mistime the catching action. They are not chosen to play and their self-esteem is damaged. And what of the children who can't join in rhythmical clapping games because they haven't the necessary control over their arms and hands? They soon get left out. Children with a poor sense of balance find running, jumping and actions like forward rolls difficult, because to be controlled and safe the body must be balanced in action. And there are other safety worries, e.g. when children go out in the traffic alone, as they could find stopping at the kerb a real problem!

And so it can be seen that if children have difficulty moving easily and confidently, they will be prevented from participating fully in many aspects of their learning – in movement activities such as running, jumping and climbing which require gross motor control (large movements carried out effectively), in 'classroom' activities such as drawing, writing, building and manipulating puzzles which require fine motor control (small movements carried out accurately), in everyday coping activities such as getting dressed and undressed which need planning ahead as well as both gross and fine movements, and in social activities where being able to play ball or skip or ride a bike, or even being able to follow the rules, means getting invited to play.

As the nursery teachers gave these descriptions, they explained that they had a number of questions, each of which will be considered in turn in the indicated chapters:

1. What are the signs and symptoms which could alert us to the children's difficulties and what are the implications of each one? (Chapter 2)

2. How can we observe and analyse the children's movements to find the specific difficulty each child has? (Chapter 3)
3. Why are the children having these difficulties? (Chapter 4)
4. What is involved in moving well? (Chapter 4)
5. How can we cope with assessing and recording when the children do all sorts of different movements? (Chapter 7)
6. What kind of activities would best help alleviate the difficulties? (Chapter 8).

Answering question 1: 'What are the signs and symptoms of movement difficulties and the implications of each one?'

The difficulties exhibited by these children form the following list. Of course, not all of the children had all of the difficulties and the level of disability was different too. All children have their unique set of characteristics. Nonetheless, there are generalities which can be made to point the way to providing help.

The first five signs, mainly concerned with perception, are as follows:

1. Poor body awareness, i.e. knowing where the body parts are in relation to one another. This causes difficulty in spatial judgments and in the timing/ coordination of actions.

(Tom, Ben and Ian)

2. Poor sense of body boundary, i.e. knowing where the body ends and the outside world begins. This causes confusion in estimating distances.

(Tom)

3. Difficulty in concentrating, i.e. being able to shut out distractors such as noises or movements. This causes poor attention span.

(Graeme)

4. Difficulty in three dimensional vision and in judging distances between objects. This causes bumping and delay in reacting to approaching objects.

(Tom)

5. Touch defensiveness, i.e. shying away from contact, over-protecting personal space, tending to be irritable if nudged.

(Graeme)

Alternatively there may be a need for heavy pressure. In this case exaggerated stepping or thumping is displayed, giving satisfaction from forceful feedback.

(Tom)

The next three relate to planning:

6. Difficulty in knowing what to do, i.e. judging what kind of response is acceptable.

(Alys)

7. Difficulty in carrying out sequences of movements, i.e. difficulty in planning ahead and remembering what comes next.

(Graeme)

8. Difficulty in generalising, i.e. adapting one learned movement to another situation.

(Alys)

The last five concern doing or executing the movements:

9. Poor postural control resulting from poor muscle tone, i.e. floppy limbs caused by poor muscle control around a joint. Poor stability and balance and as a result, difficulty in moving with control especially if speed is required.

(Ben and Ian)

10. Poor regulation in the amount of strength and speed used leading to over- or underdoing the amount of effort needed.

(Tom)

11. Lack of clear bilateral dominance, i.e. no clear picture of a stronger side. Mixed dominance leads to directional confusion.

(Graeme)

12. Ipse-lateral hand use, i.e. a tendency to use each hand on its own side of the body. Avoidance of actions which require crossing the midline.

(Ben)

13. Speech problems caused by poor control of the small muscles in the mouth.

(Alys)

Thinking back over the earlier descriptors, I hope you will recognise Tom, Ben, Graeme, Alys and Ian.

In addition some children may have retained some primal reflexes. These cause involuntary movements, e.g. shrugging, twitching, fidgeting. They prevent the development of more segmented movements.

Blythe (1992) explains that

> the continued presence of a cluster of aberrant reflexes causes writing and copying difficulties, impaired short term memory, the inability to sit still, excessive daydreaming, clumsiness and to a lesser degree mathematical problems.

Analysing observations of the children's movements in this way ensures that the most pertinent kind of help can be given, for it would not be helpful for children to practise a movement pattern if, for example, it was the planning or perhaps the ability to remember the order of sequential movements which was causing the problem.

And so the nature of difficulties has been identified. But how were these assessments made? Are they valid? Do they give an accurate picture so that help can confidently be planned? Or, if other people were making observations, would they see different things? And do observations, even carefully constructed observations, provide 'the whole story', or do contextual factors like previous experience and/or tiredness need to be considered?

Before investigating the children's difficulties further, taking a moment to reflect on the ways in which observations should be made will help to ensure that any recordings are as accurate as possible, given the transient nature of movement.

CHAPTER 3

Planning observations

Answering question 2: 'How can we observe and analyse the children's movements to find the specific difficulties each child has?'

Finding what is wrong is not easy, especially when there are lots of young children milling about and especially in the nursery when the children can mainly choose what they want to do. But of course making observations is the first step in deciding on the most beneficial kinds of activities. Before doing this, however, there are some planning considerations which will help observations to be recorded accurately. These are especially important if more than one person is to be involved in helping, or if specialist input from other professionals such as physiotherapists is likely to be requested.

Firstly, it is important that the children are observed in a number of different situations so that a range of coping or not-coping strategies are portrayed. This helps the assessor decide whether the children have a general low level of movement ability (and this may be quite different to their other profile of abilities), or whether specific kinds of tasks are problematic. As a first level observational tool, a piechart, recording exactly what each child chooses to do and what is avoided, provides an indication of where difficulties might lie (see Figure 3.1).

The teacher making this recording suspected that her child had poor leg strength and she decided to record in this kind of way to see what the exact problems were, or indeed to find whether movements which required leg strength were being avoided. When she found her suspicions confirmed, she focused on recording the leg patterns so that she could immediately select leg-strengthening exercises and also give helpful details to the physiotherapist.

Observing, recording, then observing again in this more focused and informed way may show that the child has pronounced difficulty on one side of the body and

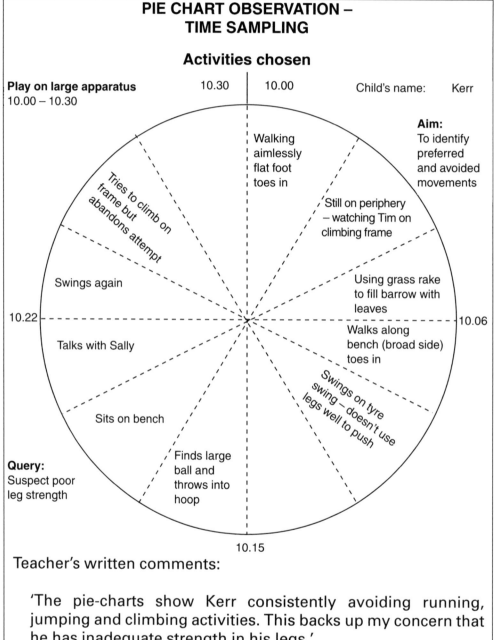

**PIE CHART OBSERVATION –
TIME SAMPLING**

Activities chosen

Play on large apparatus
10.00 – 10.30

10.30 | 10.00

Child's name: Kerr

Aim:
To identify
preferred
and avoided
movements

Walking
aimlessly
flat foot
toes in

Still on periphery
– watching Tim on
climbing frame

Tries to climb on
frame but
abandons attempt

Swings again

Using grass rake
to fill barrow with
leaves

10.22

10.06

Talks with Sally

Walks along
bench (broad side)
toes in

Swings on tyre
swing – doesn't use
legs well to push

Sits on bench

Query:
Suspect poor
leg strength

Finds large
ball and
throws into
hoop

10.15

Teacher's written comments:

'The pie-charts show Kerr consistently avoiding running, jumping and climbing activities. This backs up my concern that he has inadequate strength in his legs.'

Action: Encourage climbing on low inclined plank and on ladder. Offer support. Check if access to physiotherapist is possible.

Figure 3.1 Pie chart observation; time sampling

this would demonstrate that the other hemisphere in the brain was causing the problem. If, for example, left-side difficulties emerged and therefore right hemisphere problems were diagnosed, this might correlate with other diagnoses giving a fuller endorsement of the difficulty and justifying any plan for remediation or request for help.

It is therefore best if observations can be made in different venues so that a comprehensive picture emerges, e.g. in the home, can the children get dressed without too much difficulty, putting their clothes on in the right order or do they get into all sorts of tangles? at school, can the children draw a circle without changing the pencil from one hand to the other? when playing outside, can they run and jump without falling over? and generally, are they confident children and do they have friends? This may mean parents and teachers sharing and comparing their observations and ideally preparing helpful ways forward together. As a result, each will know that the other fully understands the child's difficulties and is taking steps to overcome them. This should also relieve the pressure of worrying if and how the other is coping. It should also make life less confusing for the children, who have just one set of guidelines to follow.

Secondly, it is important that 'usual' patterns of movement or behaviour are recorded. We all know that most children will, on occasion, play up or act out of character. Perhaps, just to give one example, they'll decide not to hear when this means interrupting a game or tidying their toys! But it is the children who seem genuinely unaware – those children who have difficulty deciphering your call from the noises round about – who need help. Similarly with bumping and dropping things. While all young children have mishaps, those who constantly fumble and spill, or who have to hold things against their chests for extra support, are the ones who need to be identified and helped.

Although it sounds quite straightforward to identify and record 'usual' movement patterns and ignore 'one-offs', children with difficulties tend not to be consistent in the quality of the movements they use. Some days are better than others and this can cause frustration for both the children and their teachers. This also means that observations have to be carried out on several occasions and the results compared to ensure they are accurate, before any claims about disability or progress can be confidently made.

Moreover, observations should be made when the children are fresh and in familiar situations. Children who take time to size up a new playground possibly teeming with noisy youngsters may just be taking sensible precautions – furthermore they may hold back because they do not relish the kinds of things on offer. Inexperienced or over-zealous observers could easily confuse this with the children 'not being able to join in'. On the other hand, the children may be reluctant to play because they don't pick up the signals telling them what the game is about; and if they can't visualise the kind of actions which would be appropriate, they are naturally afraid of intervening in an unacceptable kind of way and being rejected. And so if others have begun a game, they may want to play but hang back because they don't know how to join in! Understanding the reasoning behind the action helps clarify the assessment.

The same kind of empathy is needed for children who behave badly, perhaps being aggressive or sulky. They may have self-evaluated their own competence quite accurately and covered their disappointment and frustration by reacting in this way. Can you imagine how Reuben felt when he screamed out, 'I know what I want my hands to do but they just won't do it!' At the end of their tether, children like Reuben may lash out and spoil other children's games, for if they can't do it, then no-one else should either! And as bad behaviour usually gets attention, could this be a way of seeking help?

And so it can be seen that making accurate observations needs planning and practice, for movement is transitory and the children won't wait!

Even before making observations it's a good idea to run some checks.

1. Do the children clearly understand what it is they have to do? For some children need several explanations and some forget from day to day.
2. Is the level of task-demand appropriate for the age and stage of development of the children? Would a variety of equipment, e.g. benches broad side and narrow side up, allow them to choose and join in?
3. Would a change of equipment help? e.g. a triangular pencil grip, a work card to save copying from the board, or a bigger, softer ball?
4. Are the children motivated to carry out the set task? It can sometimes be difficult to differentiate between 'can't do' and 'doesn't want to do', but distinguishing between the two kinds of response is very important in making assessments about the children's difficulties.
5. Are there ways of minimising other distractions e.g. in school moving the child to a quieter corner of the room, or at home having a plain bedroom carpet so that dropped toys or shoes are easily seen?
6. Can picture cues help the children follow a series of instructions? This would help differentiate between 'not understanding' and 'not wanting to do'.
7. Can the children's partners be patient and kind?
8. Have the children suitable footwear? Slippy soles or inflexible trainers can really hinder competent movement, e.g. the transfer of weight from heel to toe which gives smooth forward propulsion when walking.
9. Does the child's body-build affect willingness to become involved? Finely built children may fear injury and avoid contact with children of a heavier build. And so the kind of game being played may affect participation.
10. Does any other difficulty, e.g. poor sight, hearing loss or speech difficulty, impinge on the children's performance?

The last question is very important. Especially at the start of the school year, staff may not be alerted by parents or medical services about children who have sight, hearing or speech difficulties. Their slower response may confuse the staff into thinking that they could have dyspraxia, when the delay or incorrect response is really due to their copying the child immediately beside them, rather than responding directly to instructions.

Children born with poor sight or hearing, perhaps due to prematurity, may not even realise that they have an impairment, for they may always have taken signals from the nearest source, child or adult, skilled or not. If their responses are inaccurate or late, the recognition/response of the affected children will be later still. Children with these disabilities need uninterrupted access to the teacher, possibly specialist equipment and if their impairments are holding them back, immediate referral to specialists in the relevant fields. They will suggest ways of helping as well as providing any necessary spectacles or hearing aids.

Verbal dyspraxia

One of the earlier signs that children may have a problem area is when their speech is difficult to understand. At home, parents may be able to make out what their children say, as they have gradually acclimatised to the way they communicate, or they may not be too concerned, thinking that maturation will solve the problem. On the other hand, anxious parents may have found that access to speech therapy is not possible, until a letter from a professional adds weight to their requests.

Speaking clearly requires the children to coordinate the speech apparatus, i.e. the lips, tongue, the hard palate (the roof of the mouth), and the soft palate (the tissue which closes the nasal passages to allow swallowing, blowing the nose, sucking and speaking). This uses over 100 muscles and so it is not difficult to understand how lack of control over the small muscle groups in the mouth results in very poor articulation. And if the children can't make themselves understood, then frustration sets in, possibly resulting in withdrawal or aggression, i.e. some form of unacceptable behaviour.

Before attempting to speak, the children may have had feeding difficulties, again because of lack of control over the small muscle groups in the mouth. Parents will not necessarily link the two difficulties, for the first may be coped with before the second becomes apparent, but often they do go together.

The children may have difficulty forming speech sounds at all. On the other hand they may manage single words but be overwhelmed by attempting sentences.

Listen to Marie, Peter's mum

'Peter spoke single words quite clearly, although later than usual, but somehow we weren't concerned because we thought that boys were generally late and he was such a bright wee thing. But when he started using sentences, then we really couldn't understand what was being said. It was really upsetting, because when we asked him to say it again – and we thought of all sorts of ways of getting him to do this, even pretending that we were deaf after a cold – he would repeat exactly the same sequence of sounds. He knew what he was trying to tell us. He understood the meaning of what he was saying alright, so we weren't concerned about the intellectual part, it was the articulation that was so worrying.

'Most of the time we coped as best we could, trying not to let Peter see how distressing this all was, trying to understand what he meant through interpreting his body language, but he got so tense and sometimes so furious that he had a temper tantrum. I must admit that sometimes we got angry too. When we realised that we were getting nowhere and his speech wasn't getting any clearer, we requested – no, demanded – speech therapy.

'Peter had a very difficult birth. He was a breech baby, delivered normally, and something went horribly wrong at the end. He had been deprived of oxygen, and had to be resuscitated. Whether that caused the difficulty, no-one would say, but he was kept on the at-risk register for a year.

'As I said, we shouted loud and long to get speech therapy and eventually we took part in a piece of research which was really interesting. The speech therapist was very enthusiastic, if very frank. He told us that Peter's vowels and consonants were all mixed up, and to try to correct this he started Peter on single sounds. I think he began with "t", and he had a little floor game which had lots of objects and he had to jump on all the ones starting with "t" saying the sound as he went. That was fun and so we were able to reinforce that learning whenever we could in the day. We practised many letters like that and then Peter had to recognise whether the sound came from the front or the back of his mouth. I think this helped him concentrate on shaping the sounds, because he gradually knew the muscles he had to use.

'Over the next two years his speech improved, slowly at first, but as his confidence grew he wanted to play the games over and over, because he knew he could do them. When he went to nursery, we could make out most of what he said although he always spoke very quietly. Of course he had realised that something about his speech was troubling us and he remains a quiet, shy child, but maybe he would have been like that anyway.

'When he went to "big school" he had a tremendous surprise. He knew all his sounds. The speech therapy games had taught him the basics of reading. In turn that helped his confidence, so we had got over the worst of the problem and there was an unexpected bonus. That was tremendous!'

So when any kind of difficulties are severe, specialist help is essential, along with parental commitment to keep the remedial programme going. Communication with the school staff is essential too, for there are many things which can be done to ease the children's day, e.g. giving them the time they need to speak and ensuring that conversations happen in a quiet spot, not asking the children to speak in front of others until they say they are ready, and whenever possible not asking for repetitions. This may involve learning to read the children's body language or, for children with severe difficulties, their signing patterns.

In other words, there are common-sense steps which seem obvious but which can be overlooked when there are thirty or so other children needing attention too! But only when all of these different aspects of the children's performance have been considered can observers confidently claim that no other variables have distorted their recordings. This being so, they can form part of each child's assessment profile.

When observing children moving, it is also important to remember that while some children with difficulties can do everyday practised movements quite well, they may not generalise their learning, i.e. they have difficulty adapting a learned pattern to a new situation. Rush (1997) tells of one child who, on learning to swim, asked her teacher, 'Now can you teach me to swim in my pool?' This child thought she would have to learn from scratch again! She didn't realise that she could transfer her new skill to another environment. This is why some children with movement difficulties 'have a very tiring day' (British Child Health and Education Study 1985). They 'have to work much harder than other children.' (Chesson *et al.* 1990) and become understandably tired and cross. They have to approach each action as if it were a first-time try and concentrate when other children are moving easily, apparently without thought. And so observations should encompass both practised and first-time tries.

Appreciating these problems has implications for teaching, Firstly, in deciding on the number and complexity of new things that children should be asked to do; and secondly in taking care that the environment does not add unnecessary difficulty. Above all, teachers and nursery nurses really need to understand the children's difficulties and not unwittingly make things worse, e.g. by offering rewards when the children are already trying as hard as they can!

Sometimes talking with the children can provide another level of explanation of their difficulties, but interactions need to be positive and open-ended with no sense of criticism or blame! 'I'll bet you enjoyed your snack today' may elicit the response that the child did or did not spill, and even lead to a suggestion of practice, whereas even a smiling, 'Did you spill your juice?' implies that the child has disappointed, and is not likely to promote further conversation. Focusing on things the children can do and enjoy doing also helps to keep their difficulties in perspective, for if they mainly reflect on the things that were difficult and see these as insurmountable barriers, it is easy for them to become overwhelmed by feelings of inadequacy and stop trying. Another coping strategy is for some children to adopt an air of bravado to cover their feelings of inadequacy, e.g. saying 'Who would want to do that anyway?' All may not be as it seems.

One useful interaction strategy is to try to think ahead and imagine the kinds of input you will make in a conversation and about the responses which are likely to emerge. If one-word replies are likely, then reconsidering the prompt is a good idea, for we all know that the answer to 'What did you do at school today?' is likely to be 'nothing' despite the teachers' best efforts to help the children learn!

An adult comment on a childhood experience often stimulates the children's language more than questions which can be answered 'yes' or 'no' or even be ignored.

An example may help. In this scenario, the teacher, Mark, was aware that the child had just returned from holiday at the seaside and he was trying to avoid the usual, 'What did you do?', 'What did you see?' kind of questions which could have elicited a one-word reply. He anticipated Jon building castles in the wet sand tray to help strengthen his hands.

M: I remember going to the seaside when I was little . . .

J: Were you ever little?

M: (recovering), Well, when I was about six, I built lots of castles . . .

J: That's for babies. I go on boats and see the seals and they're grey and have whiskers . . . and there's a big flashing light.

M: I think that's a warning light . . .

J: A what? It isn't you know, it's to stop boats crashing onto the rocks . . .

M: Tell me about that . . . Would you like to hear a story about a lighthouse now? [*The Lighthouse-keeper's lunch*]

M = Mark, the teacher; J = Jon, the child.

Mark was nearly floored by the child's amazed interjection, 'Were you ever little?' but he persevered and found that the child, previously quite abrupt and reluctant to chat, was ready to share recent experiences with marked confidence. This interaction also gave the teacher clues as to the child's interests and helped him plan learning activities which would be likely to encourage the child to communicate.

A small group listened to the story and then made a lighthouse out of kitchen junk and a basket of plasticine food, which the children thought the lighthouse-keeper would enjoy. This led to discussions about lighthouses, where they were to be found and what the children thought about staying for so long in one, isolated place. Seagulls and their acquisition of food were another enthusiastic, if rather gory, topic of conversation.

Making the food involved much rolling, shaping and flattening new plasticine which needed firm handling. This was a deliberate ploy to provide resistance/ strengthening work for Jon's hands.

Those who research into the development of talk, e.g. Wood (1992), advise teachers to let children initiate the conversations if they will, because as their interests become apparent, it becomes easier to prolong a meaningful and logical interaction. Certainly the sea-chat conversations were illuminating, the subsequent activities really motivating for the children and the clay was ideal for strengthening the poor muscle tone in Jon's hands.

Neither recording nor interpreting observations of children and interactions with them is easy; the strategy is time-consuming, but practice does help. Moreover, the recordings provide evidence of what is happening in the children's day and as such are a rich source of evidence for helping the children in the most appropriate way. Over time, they provide a record of the children's progress which is vitally important for their parents, for new teachers and for when the children move to a new environment. Informed, the 'new' carers can immediately empathise with the children's difficulties and consider, ahead-of-time, ways of alleviating them.

CHAPTER 4

Movement learning

Answering question 3: 'Why are the children having difficulties?'

You will have noticed that the list of difficulties in Chapter 2 is subdivided into three groupings with 'perception', 'planning/organising' and 'executing or doing' as titles heading each part. This is because moving well, i.e. efficiently and appropriately in different environments, depends on all three:

- *perception* the ability to recognise, interpret and process sensory stimuli from the environment;
- *planning* the ability to build a mental model, i.e. to know what to do;
- *organising* the ability to memorise patterns of sequential movements; and
- *executing* the ability to carry out the movements themselves.

When children move, they make a series of perceptual-motor decisions. These are based on the information coming from the environment through the senses which is then interpreted in the brain. In turn, this is relayed to the muscles and joints and they are stimulated to give a movement response. If the central nervous system does not do this adequately, then the acquisition and development of movement skills will be delayed.

To be able to move well, without fumbling or stumbling, the perceptual input from the different senses must be accurate and the processing mechanism sound. If either inaccurate or inadequate perceptual information starts off the process, then the ensuing interpretation will be flawed. At the interpretation stage, there are two kinds of problems. Some children may not be able to plan what kind of actions are appropriate, but for many more the organisation is the real stumbling block. These children know, intellectually, what they want to do, but lack the movement memory which would allow them to organise their movement patterns appropriately. And finally, at the execution stage, the children must have the movement abilities, i.e. the coordination, balance strength and body awareness, to fulfil the instructions which are received.

The three parts can also be viewed as an input–output map (see Figure 4.1) and this brings in the concept of feedback.

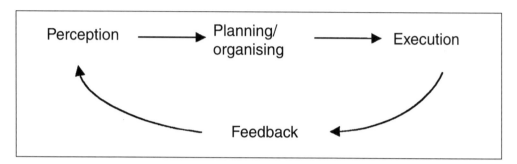

Figure 4.1 An input–output model

The feedback loop shown in the diagram is an important part of the process, which is really cyclical, not linear. This means that the imprint of a movement pattern is stored in the memory, retrieved, then used as a basis for further learning when a similar, more challenging movement is attempted. If the original has been poorly constructed, then subsequent attempts have a faulty recipe and the resulting movement patterns are impaired.

This explains why practice alone will not necessarily improve performance, for unless the movement patterns are correct, the children will just get faster at doing the wrong thing!

Each of the three sub-components will now be explained in greater detail, and then some suggestions to alleviate difficulties will be made. Figure 4.2 sets out the five aspects of perception to be considered.

Perception: the senses and the part they play in moving well

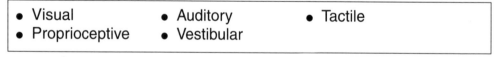

Figure 4.2 The senses

Visual

The most obvious visual aid is being able to see clearly and therefore being able to recognise people and objects and the distances between them. To do this the eyes must work together. Children with visual difficulties may screw up one eye or hold their head to the side or shake their heads to try to clear their vision. They can become very tired struggling to bring things into focus. Opticians may not find that there is a sight problem per se – but assessment of their functional vision may tell a different story.

If there is faulty visual tracking, following the flight path of a ball may be difficult, and if it is, then the preparation for catching has to be rushed and the catch won't be cleanly made. Fingers will fumble if the ball isn't missed altogether, not because the children can't catch but because they don't see the approaching ball in time to make the necessary adjustments. Visual tracking also influences reading ability, as the eyes must follow the sequence of letters smoothly from left to right. If they jump or miss letters, sounding them out makes no sense!

Once the children are into the primary classroom their difficulties become more apparent. Learning to read is often unexpectedly problematic once there are several words in a line and several lines on a page. Then faulty tracking causes the eyes to jump lines, or alternatively, the inability to focus means that letters run together on the page. And similarly with mathematics: visual difficulties can cause mathematical 'errors' if the rows and columns of figures swim together out of line. And so while children can understand the meaning and the technique, they are unable to provide the correct written answer.

The most problematic task of all can be copying from the board especially if there are several sets of instructions written there. Think of what this involves. First the children have to identify where their own instructions are midst all the others – then find the correct place in their jotter. By the time their eyes go back to the board, the lines are blurring. Then they must transpose a set of symbols from one to the other and take them from the vertical to the horizontal. This is difficult enough if the symbols make logical sense, because in that case the storyline can be remembered, but if there are shapes or numbers which in themselves have no meaning the task difficulty is much greater. If this transposing has to be done many times it is no wonder that the children can become frantic!

Another difficulty can be poor three-dimensional vision. This may prevent the children appreciating that objects jut out in their path and so they get bumped and bruised. Judging distances between objects will also be affected. Dropping things is usual because the children don't accurately estimate the distance between e.g. the cup of juice and the table. These children have difficulty seeing objects as distinct from their background – hence the children who cannot find their shoes on a patterned carpet or who find charts and maps difficult to read. Witkin (Witkin and Goodenough 1981) called this perceptual ability, field-dependence/field-independence. He described how children and adults had different visual cues, for, while those who had field-dependent vision saw things rather flat and undifferentiated and needed time to distinguish e.g. an approaching ball from the background or a car approaching round a corner, those with field-independent sight had a clear picture much earlier, allowing them to make the appropriate judgments to make the catch deft, or to wait on the pavement, or to move around the classroom without bumping into the furniture.

Holding eye contact can be another stumbling block, for some children have difficulty estimating the kind of eye contact which promotes social interaction. They either avoid looking directly, and this gives the impression that they are not interested, or they hold for too long and the other children feel uncomfortable and move away to protect their personal space. This can really work against the affected children making friends, and of course they can't understand why.

Some children with perception problems have two difficulties. They can't bear their personal space to be invaded and, as they may also misjudge distances, they may overreact to the perceived invasion of their space by children who have no such intention. Another distressing outcome!

Some children are too easily distracted by the movements of other children around them or e.g. leaves blowing on the tree outside. They can't screen out these movements and so look away from the task at hand, fix their attention elsewhere and get scolded for not paying attention. But this is a visual problem, not really inattention.

All of these children have a real difficulty and they are not being naughty.

What can be done to help?
It can be difficult to identify just what is wrong, especially in group work in the class when children work out strategies for themselves. 'Not to worry,' said Liam. 'Maths is fine. Calum always checks my answers for we don't want to lose group points!' However, parents and teachers are not likely to be so easily satisfied, and, being concerned that the children's oral work is much better than their written, will soon be making the kinds of assessments which will differentiate between the two abilities. They will then be able, perhaps, to provide more opportunities for oral work across the curriculum, thus reducing the reading/writing/copying stress.

To help three-dimensional difficulties in young children, getting them to feel solid blocks, maybe counting the corners, can help, i.e. using sensitive touch as a helping mechanism. In the nursery, brightly coloured plastic chairs can be more easily seen and cause less bruising. And of course all sharp corners will be removed already. Using plain backgrounds for wall mountings and non-patterned boxes to hold pencils and crayons will help the children retrieve them quickly, and let them begin in time.

Colour-coding helps identification of nearly everything. Colour-coding on the board and in the jotter telling the children where to start and where to finish can be a great help. Using the children's favourite colour to colour-code pegs in the cloakroom is another simple ploy which can give a positive start to the day.

Thinking through the children's day, and finding where even simple measures like colour coding can help, is initially very time-consuming but it saves time and frustration later in repeating instructions or eventually doing the job for the children who are then made to feel inadequate.

When children with visual difficulties read, they may need a card underlining the correct line for much longer than the children without problems. Some children's books with larger size text can help too because there are fewer words on the page. The children can then read the same story as their friends and progress through the book quite quickly which is encouraging. And if easily distracted children can have their backs to windows where people pass, or where branches wave, then the number of distractors is reduced. Sum jotters with large boxes, worksheets blown up on the photocopier and robust toys in bright colours are all good ideas. Dressing up in large-size play clothes can allow children to practise everyday coping skills without any time pressure, so buttons may get done and laces may be tied.

In the playground or in the gym, larger softer balls travel more slowly and give time for adjustments to be made. In ball games, the distance between thrower and catcher needs to be gauged carefully – too close and there is no time, too far away and the tracking becomes impossible. Hedgehog balls, i.e. those with soft rubber spikes, make catching easier and bean-bags land on the spot and don't need chasing and so make useful alternatives to rubber balls.

Thus there are many things which can be done to ease the day and let the children experience success.

Auditory

Hearing clearly allows children to be alert to everything that is going on around and so they can act quickly on the basis of that information. Difficulty in listening means that responding is likely to be delayed – not a popular reaction in school or at home when parents are rushed. But why should this be, especially when audiologists discern no hearing loss?

Some children find it difficult, even impossible, to filter out 'other' noises in their environment. All day they are trying to listen through other sounds – again a real reason for being tired. Relief comes from switching off which can be a survival mechanism. When teachers say 'He is in a world of his own', this could be the reason why.

If sounds are not sharp, the children may not hear the rhythm of a movement pattern, and differentiating between the hard and soft beats can help prepare a mental image of the action which is a kind of rehearsal of the movement itself. The easiest adult example of this would be hearing the rhythm of the hop, step and jump, for listening even without seeing can convey whether the take-off is strong enough and discern the length of time taken for each phase and therefore whether the jump is long. With young children, learning to skip is helped by listening to the rhythm of the step pattern as well as watching, and trying, preferably hand in hand with someone who can skip.

And what of safety? Not hearing approaching traffic encourages children to rush across the road, and not hearing an approaching object and taking avoiding action may mean a sore bump. During group work, children with this kind of difficulty may not hear the teacher's instructions above the chatter and be startled by the sudden movement of the others, causing them to react inappropriately.

What can be done to help?
Again modifying the environment to take note of the difficulties of noise-sensitive children is the best way to help. Ensuring that there is a quiet space for retreating and playing, as well as reading stories and having 'quiet as a mouse games' like stalking allow concentration and fun. Simple clapping games with a partner will be enjoyed by some children. Explanations should be kept short and be given at a time when there is minimum noise – and repeating instructions when this is not necessary should be avoided. This is all to make it easier for the children to hear.

Perhaps the other children could be encouraged to be quieter if the teacher interacts as a role model, using gestures instead of speech? Perhaps most helpful of all are one-to-one teaching opportunities when the duo can talk clearly and quietly, thus avoiding the difficulties which may arise within larger groups.

Tactile

This is a very interesting sense with important if less obvious implications for children struggling to move well. Some children just can't bear to be touched and react very strongly, in the worst cases violently, to even a light touch. And because children with movement difficulties tend to respond to instructions rather slowly, other children may 'encourage' them by prodding or poking. The touch-sensitive children may well overreact. Being nudged in the queue or even inadvertently bumped can cause children to flail out. Other children naturally resent this. It has real social disadvantages, for who is going to choose a partner who is unpredictable when the teacher says, 'take hands'?

On the other hand, some children need to have strong feedback from the environment to allow them to feel secure when moving. These are the children who thump around, heavy-footed rather than fleet of foot! They hold their pencil tightly and press heavily and if the lead doesn't immediately break, then the writing is messy and black. They pull their laces too tightly and they snap; they pour the juice too fiercely and it spills all over the place. They knock into their seat as they stand up and the chair clatters over. You can imagine the response, yet the children may not know what is amiss or be able to modify their behaviour. Parents and teachers say, 'They don't know their own strength!' and this is true and the source of much distress when other children's toys are broken. You can hear their cry: 'I didn't do it, it just broke!'

Socially, some timid children will shy away from those who bump, while others find the effects funny and laugh, unwittingly or even knowingly reinforcing the fracas!

What can be done to help?

As these children enjoy reactive pressure, they will relish playing with clay or moulding plasticine – activities that require physical pressure to be successful. In the nursery, building large bricks or hammering nails are popular choices, although while they are satisfying, they are not going to help the problem. As a contrast, blowing to keep feathers up in the air or similar gentle activities like stroking the hamster (supervised!), or 'stalking through the forest without waking the giant', are enjoyable games, the last of which promotes careful placing of the foot on the floor in a heel–toe action which holds back the pressure, and slows the pace. Feelie bag games where the children attempt to recognise objects by their feel, i.e. their shape and size, without seeing, encourage gentle handling while games like spilikins encourage use of the pincer grip and taking time to be precise!

Outdoors, imaginative games which have running then slowing down 'before you fall in the (rope) river', help children feel the 'slowing down to stop' movement which is very important, linking as it does to safety on the road, running towards the chute in the swing park or any activity which needs changes of speed and whole body control. These kinds of activities help the children learn that they can move around quietly, that 'clatter-bang' can be avoided and more friends can be made.

Proprioceptive

The proprioceptor cells which are in the muscles and joints of the body work with the kinesthetic groups to tell where the body is in relation to outside objects. They help movement to be segmented and efficient. Children who have a sound proprioceptive sense can sit down without looking at the chair – they sense where it is, how high the seat is and therefore accurately gauge the amount of effort needed to sit down. They can do all their usual movement patterns without looking – fastening their coats, even fastening buttons can be done by feel alone. Those who can't must compensate by turning to see and/or bending to feel, i.e. movements which take time and need added coordination. Proprioceptors also help maintain balance and control, especially when different amounts of fluctuating strength are required, e.g. in bicycling over uneven grass instead of on a smooth pathway. Children with a poor proprioceptive sense are less skilled in these types of movements and need to use their other senses, particularly visual, to compensate.

Vestibular

Vestibular receptors are situated in the inner ear and work to coordinate movements which require balance. This is why children with an ear infection often find their sense of balance is affected and find usual movements like walking problematic. Many children however, actually seek out similar feelings. They love to go on the waltzer at the fair. The whirling action temporarily confuses their vestibular receptors and they feel giddy, almost out of control. Others find this kind of sensation unpleasant, to be avoided at all costs! But even those who seek this temporary sensation of vertigo would not wish to have it continuously, because maintaining balance would then be extremely stressful.

The vestibular sense responds to changes of position of the head, automatically coordinating the eyes and body. It helps children realise the midline of their bodies which is important in understanding directionality.

All of these senses work together to enable children to be efficient and effective movers. The most important thing is that parents, teachers and nursery nurses recognise the difficulties which these children endure. When they do, they will realise the importance of praising for effort rather than outcome, and hopefully this will be the best confidence-giver of all.

(Other senses, e.g. kinesthetic, balance, coordination, rhythm and reaction time, will be covered under 'Movement abilities', p. 53–68).

Planning and organisation

The second aspect of moving well comes under the heading of 'planning and organising'. There is a subtle difference which can cause observers to make an incorrect diagnosis. Some children will not be able to build a mental model – they won't know what it is they want to do. They have a planning deficit. This prevents them carrying out sequences of movements because they can't visualise what comes next. And if they can't anticipate the outcome of movements, then they are unable to evaluate the wisdom of doing the movements at all. Safety worries are paramount for children like this.

Other children can plan, they can describe what they wish to do, but they do not have the movement memory or organisational skills to carry it out. And so they are likely to do things in the wrong order, e.g. they know they have to get dressed, but put trousers on before pants or shoes before socks. This is sometimes called ideational dyspraxia. Any kind of timetabling/structure to the day is difficult for these children. Getting organised in school – finding a jotter, taking it to a desk, identifying a work card and choosing a sharp pencil – can be guided by a sympathetic teacher, but finding the way unsupervised from one room to another is really problematic. Many children with this difficulty also appear to have no sense of time and so 'Be ready in five minutes' or any kind of 'Let's do this first and then that later' is not understood in the sequence of time sense.

Digue and Kettles (1996) explain that the children's difficulties are in completing complex tasks, i.e. those involving set response sequences such as those found in all the activities of daily living. They write that

> these children face immense difficulties as most complex tasks have many components that are automatically carried out in the correct sequence, and frequently simultaneously.

Think of the children coming for their snack. Finding their names, donning aprons, finding a space and sitting down, cutting food and pouring juice and all the time watching the child in the next chair. It's a wonder they can do it at all! People who can move easily take so much for granted. This is why teachers and nursery nurses have to understand the analysis of movement. Those who fail to appreciate the organisational difficulties these children have can easily become irritated. 'They never know where they are going', 'always lagging behind', 'totally disorganised', are usual, if unkind and less than helpful, descriptors.

What can be done to help?
At the conceptualisation stage, talking with the children, asking 'What is it that you would like to do?', can tell whether the children have ideas and plans as a basis for acting. Observing the children carefully to see whether they are waiting and copying rather than following some plan of their own is a useful ploy. It is important that adults recognise the difference between the two kinds of problem because suggesting ideas to children who already know what they want to do is confusing and dispiriting if they feel constrained to jettison their own plans. Much better if teachers discover the children's plans if they have them and then say 'Right, now let's work out how we are going to manage that' and support the children as they try. One is helping with ideas, the other with organisational strategies to carry them out. Needless to say, both should be done in a positive, helpful manner, using as much of the children's input as possible. One of the hardest teaching jobs is to learn to listen and not take over from a slower child, because this takes the joy of achievement away.

Examples
'Show me the basket that is going to catch the ball. Is it strong? Where are your elbows? In to your sides? Feel them pressing? Make sure your fingers are close together so that the ball doesn't slip through. Now you are ready. Watch the ball. Well done.'

'Let me hold your coat. Now where is your arm going to go? Can you shoot your fingers through? Can you feel them? Wiggle them if you can!'

In these kinds of learning experiences the teachers are breaking down the tasks and doing much of the work of ordering the activity. This kind of input helps the children remember the correct sequence of events. This helps body awareness and body boundary. The children are also being asked to feel where their body parts are, even when they are out of sight. This should help them develop a sense of first, second and third and, through identifying the function of the different body parts, help their body awareness and make them less dependent on visual cues.

Execution: carrying out the movement

In the research the parents and teachers explained that, although they could spot a child having difficulty, they were unsure of what was involved in analysing the movement patterns as a preparation for helping.

This part looks at movement analysis in detail. The first thing would be to understand the types of the different kinds of movements and the demands they make, particularly for children experiencing problems.

Movements can be subdivided into:

1. gross and fine movements
2. habitual and non-habitual movements
3. automatic and voluntary movements
4. closed and open skills
5. manipulative skills.

1. Gross and fine movements

Gross movements use the large muscle groups which work together to produce actions such as walking, running, jumping and climbing. They need a good deal of strength, control and whole body coordination. The demands made by fine movements are different – speaking, eating, writing and playing the piano are examples that show that only small body parts are used. In young children, gross movements involving balance and coordination of the large muscle groups are developed first. This explains why some children can run yet are unable to control a pencil. And of course children have been practising these large movements longer!

Fine motor skills come later yet sometimes they are easier, because when one part of the body is 'fixed', as in sitting, it does not need to be controlled and full concentration can go to the moving parts. But of course fine movements can be very intricate, involving hand–eye coordination (e.g. cutting food, threading beads) or requiring greater rhythmical awareness (e.g. in playing the piano) or significant control in a small area (e.g. in writing, colouring-in or speaking).

This sequence of development, i.e. gross then fine movements, also explains why children's difficulties may not be apparent in the earliest months. Parents can miss fine motor skill difficulties because they assume that because the gross motor skills are achieved, the fine motor skills will be proficient as well.

2. Habitual and non-habitual movements

Habitual movements are grooved, everyday movements which have been refined through daily practice. Because of the practice element and because others are likely to be acting as role models, children with movement difficulties learn to carry out these movements adequately, although probably at the lower level of competence (Ayres 1972).

Non-habitual movements – e.g. coming down a stairway with unusual spacing between the steps, walking over rough ground, sliding on ice – these kinds of movements are likely to be problematic because coping means adjusting the usual pattern of the movement and dealing with non-practised elements. Children with movement difficulties find the adjustments taxing and may act like a much younger child, e.g. needing a hand and/or using a 'one-foot leading, step-together' pattern on the stair. The child's body posture may change – stooping forward with tense shoulders because of enlisting visual cues instead of relying on proprioceptors to relay the correct messages to the brain. And so the movement has become a whole-body movement, needing whole-body control rather than segmented actions which show a more mature level of presentation.

3. Automatic and voluntary movements

Automatic movements are controlled by the cerebellum, and even complex actions are carried out without apparent thought, but strangely enough, when the same action comes under voluntary control, it can be much more problematic. An adult example may help. Think of learning to type. Suddenly, spelling which has been easily and correctly achieved at the automatic level becomes a problem. Even simple, straightforward words cause hesitations and doubts. This is because the normal rhythm of the spelling has been displaced by the slower typing and so brought from the automatic to the level of conscious thought.

And similarly with children. One day they will come into school and effortlessly bring out the correct book and begin to write. They have been stimulated by the sight of the book and followed a practised routine automatically. But when their teacher gives them the same sequence of instructions, e.g. 'Do this . . . fetch this, do that . . .' then it involves planning and organising voluntary movements at a conscious level which can be overwhelming. So, those who do not understand wonder, 'If he can manage one day, why not the next?' This is one reason why!

4. Open and closed skills

Another, in some ways similar method of analysis is in terms of 'open and closed skills'. Closed skills are similar to habitual movements in that the same pattern is replicated, but the terminology also means that the environment is involved. So, whereas a closed skill in a closed environment could be swimming a practised stroke in a known swimming pool where the demands of the environment are relatively unchanging, swimming to keep afloat in a rough sea would mean that both the skill and the environment were unpredictable and so coping would require constant adjustment, according to the height of the waves and/or any floating debris or jellyfish! The swimmer would then need open skills in an open environment, a much more difficult challenge.

Early-years children encounter the same kind of changing demands when they go on outings, maybe travelling on a bus to the zoo. Coping with a shoogly, juddering bus (when they usually come to school by car) and not knowing the layout of the zoo or the routine of the day and where the toilets will be – will there be toilets? – can cause children to regress to a younger coping or non-coping style. They are being asked to use open skills in an open environment. Tears and wet pants show the stress. Surprises are sometimes not the treat they are meant to be!

What can be done to help?
Children with movement difficulties can be helped by knowing the routine and the expectations of the day in advance. In the nursery, before the zoo outing, perhaps the youngsters could make a 'bus' and sing, 'The boys on the bus' using swaying actions to anticipate the shoogle! And the primaries could look at enlarged maps which help familiarise the routes and point out the place for lunch break and the toilets!

While all of this may sound quite unnecessarily complex, anticipating the demands of the day like this can pinpoint where difficulties could be reduced, namely by teaching any activity as a closed skill in a closed environment until confidence is gained and adjustments can be made. Sympathetic teachers would not wish to burden children with new, open skills in open environments, unless they knew that the challenge was attainable.

One mum, Susan, was distressed because her son, Jake, didn't like other children coming to play, because 'They always spoil my game!' Jake had formulated the rules of his game in advance and had visualised what was going to happen. The anticipated game was something he knew he could do well – a closed skill in a closed (or familiar and safe) environment. But when the other children took over the game, when they changed the format and the rules, then he was into unknown territory. He could no longer anticipate what was going to happen. Jake was now facing the prospect of needing open or non-habitual skills in an open environment and, being bright, he suspected he wouldn't be able to cope.

In analysing movement, it is useful to consider the demands of the task in this kind of way and then if the children have difficulty or are unhappy or reluctant to try, to find ways in which the task demands can be reduced. This might be done by isolating the required skill and establishing it in a closed environment where the parameters of the task stay the same before putting it back into a real-life situation.

Susan also explained, 'When he's at home, he doesn't seem to be worried that he is always playing alone, he seems reasonably content or maybe he reckons that the alternative is worse. Sometimes I think I worry more for him than he does for himself.' Susan was concerned that the anxiety stemming from her own social expectations could be transferred to Jake, making his plight worse. And yet she felt he should be playing with other children. Not an easy dilemma to solve.

Bee (1998) advises that the children's interests are the bonding factors in forming friendships, rather than who the children are or parents choosing children they think might be sympathetic, allowing their children to play together. And so finding other children who are genuinely interested in the same kinds of activities could be the most helpful way forward.

5. Manipulative skills

Manipulative skills require the children to cope with outside objects, e.g. pencils, bats, plasticine, coats, knives and forks. They need to cope with the added control demands – added length and weight, flexibility or rigidity. And of course they have to make that object work, so fine motor control at the extremities is required. In writing, for example, the pencil must be manipulated out there where control is difficult. It cannot be held against the body for extra support. And if a bat is the object, then there is the added complication of tracking a ball, making contact and propelling it in the right direction. Using a shuttlecock instead is an example of reducing the demands of a task because the shuttlecock is lighter (needing less strength), it moves more slowly (requiring slower reaction time), and if it falls, it stays put (avoiding the tracking and chasing and possibly bumping which could happen in retrieving a ball). And if the hitting can be practised solo, hitting up in the air rather than to a partner, then the feel of the shuttlecock on the bat aids gauging the pressure and the rhythm, and so reduces the new demands which will come when hitting back to a partner has to be accomplished.

In activities like writing too, preliminary aids like sitting securely at the right height of desk, having a triangular pencil grip to give easier control, having guiding lines or firm paper for those that press too hard, are all strategies to make life that little bit easier and success more likely to be achieved.

Digue and Kettles (1996) highlight an important issue regarding helping children learn manipulative skills. They claim that children have great difficulty in using their hands to copy movements shown to them. As a result fine motor skills, e.g. writing, colouring-in, using a fork and knife, stay as difficult skills even when many demonstrations have been made. And so great patience and appreciation of the complexity of actions requiring control and coordination is required.

Important too is the position of the teacher. Sitting alongside rather than facing the children is best, because this saves them reversing the demonstration and 'untangling' the mirror image. And of course special help is needed for left-handed children.

Children with difficulties in any of these kinds of movements have problems knowing:

- what to move, because their body awareness is poorly developed;
- when to move, because of timing difficulties;
- how to move, because of the difficulty in selecting the correct amount of strength and speed; and
- where to move because of spatial orientation problems.

This kind of analysis was originally designed by Laban in 1942.

Let's look at how these decisions influence the efficiency of movement. See, for example, Figure 4.3.

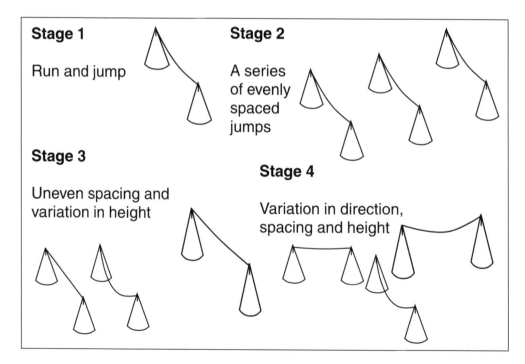

Figure 4.3 Stages in running and jumping

What kind of movement decisions need to be made if the children are to enjoy this activity? The first decision is how fast to run. If the approach to the cane is too slow, then there won't be enough momentum to lift the body into the stride-jump action, but if it is too fast, then the run goes on where the jump should be. The second concerns the amount of strength in the jump – too little and the cane won't be cleared, too much and there will be too much height or distance which makes the landing difficult to control and use as a preparation for the next run. Then decisions about which body parts to use have to be made. Are high arms really necessary in a low jump? Which foot should lead, and how many steps between each cane are needed if the same foot is to lead again? And distance decisions. How far should the take-off be from the cane and is this the same if the height of the cane varies?

All these decisions become even more complex if the canes are at irregular distances, varying heights and in different directions (see Figure 4.3). So variety should only be added once the basic running and jumping have been mastered. This is another example of moving from a closed to an open skill.

Most children will try out movements and through teaching and practice get them right, and these satisfactory patterns will be stored in their movement memory and be retrieved when similar movements are to be attempted. Children with dyspraxia lack this ability to transfer earlier learning to new situations (Ayres 1972), and so have to begin the decision-making process afresh each time they wish to try something new. Sometimes they are just too tired to try.

Answering question 4: 'What is involved in moving well?'

Analysing a movement pattern

Every movement, large or small, has three parts (see Figure 4.4).

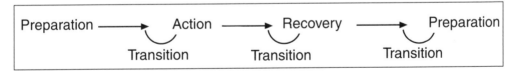

Figure 4.4 Analysis of a movement pattern

When movement is smooth and efficient, i.e. when it is well done, the three parts flow together and the momentum from one part carries on to help the next. In sequential movements, the recovery from the first blends with the preparation for the second so that there is no break.

In efficient movement, the preparatory phase 'gets the body ready' by deciding on the speed that will be needed, the direction of travel, the parts of the body to be used and the sequence of the action. The key words for the action phase are 'balance', 'control' and 'coordination'. At the end of the action there will be a release of strength so that the recovery can be resilient and lead into the next preparation. The recovery must also sustain the balance and control so that it doesn't throw the next action awry.

Flowing movement has an in-built rhythm and an awareness of this can clarify the pattern, e.g. where the strong parts need to come, and so help the pattern to be done well. Children can be helped to 'listen' for the rhythm, then clap or stamp it out. This is very good for children who have difficulty listening, for it helps them visualise a successful movement pattern.

It can be quite difficult for observers to distinguish between the three phases of a movement, especially if it is done quickly. And sometimes the difficulty lies in the transitions, i.e. the links between each part, for at these times adjustments have to be made. These involve kinesthetically anticipating the next part of the action and reacting to the demands of the movement and the environment, usually quickly. Perhaps the children need to realise that they have to get their feet ready to change direction, or if e.g. they have done a forward roll and want to get back to their feet, they have to retain a rounded shape to keep the momentum going rather than flattening out and finishing the action lying on the ground!

As the actual patterns are carried out, the children are making decisions about

1. the speed of the movement, i.e. very quick – quick – medium paced – slow – very slow
2. the strength of the movement, i.e. very strong – medium strength – delicate – fine
3. the space the movement needs, i.e. wide – narrow – direct or flexible
4. the direction of the movement, i.e. forwards – backwards – diagonally – in a curve – zig-zag
5. the flow of the movement, i.e. tightly held – jerky – smooth – free flowing.

These movement factors should be analysed by the observers too.

The wrong selection is likely to be clearly demonstrated if you watch a three to five year old girl trying to throw a ball. The first thing is that the stance is likely to show that the leading foot is on the same side as the throwing arm. This means that there can be no turn of the body and no propulsion by the throwing arm and so the throw stays as a 'poke'. The wrong preparation influences the 'action' because the stance leaves no room for the arm to swing back, and so the elbow leads into the throw. But hardest of all for this young child is the moment of releasing the ball. She uses too much strength to grip, her fingers are curled tightly round the ball, the hand opens too late and the ball dribbles down to land at her feet. You can see that if the first part of the action sequence is faulty, the whole action falls apart.

Of course the teacher must know the component parts of an effective throw so that the diagnosis can be accurate and the remediation helpful.

CHAPTER 5

Movement abilities

Some very important abilities come into play as children attempt to move well in different environments. All those who wish to help children improve their movement need to understand what they are and how they contribute to the children's acquisition of skill.

Kinesthetic awareness, balance, coordination, rhythm and speed of movement

Kinesthetic awareness

Kinesics is the study of the orientation of the body in space. Kinesthesia describes a combination of information from the senses which gives a conscious awareness of one's orientation in space. The subdivisions of kinesthetic awareness are given in Figure 5.1 and we will look at these in the following sections.

Body awareness
Spatial awareness   } Kinesthetic sense
Directionality
Body boundary

Figure 5.1 The subdivisions of kinesthetic awareness

Body awareness
Some children have very little awareness of their body parts – what they are, where they are, and how moving one part affects the others. Young children do tend to use whole body movements to accomplish a task, but gradually these become

segmented or refined so that the body parts can move in isolation with no extraneous movement. This is how moving becomes more efficient.

If it doesn't, then movements are clumsy and uncoordinated and everyday coping skills like getting dressed take ages, if they can be done at all. Holding up a jacket with one hand and finding the sleeve with the other is tricky and takes time when you aren't sure where your hand is or where it is to go! Another example of this development of isolated movement could be picking up a small object from a table. Gradually, this becomes a matter of finger dexterity, i.e. using the pincer grip, rather than whole-hand grasping, which usually means that the action is cumbersome.

Spatial awareness
This ability helps children know where they are in space, and so enables them to judge the distances between their bodies and objects in the environment around them. If this is poorly developed then e.g. feet trip going up stairs because of misjudging the height of the riser, or the ball sails past because the hands have stretched out to the wrong place. Think of children trying to place an object on a table – they perceive the table as being further or nearer than it really is, and the object either clatters down or lands on the floor! Stumbling and falling are par for the course for these children. Their teachers describe them as 'ungainly' and 'awkward' and they are never chosen to do jobs that need precision! One teacher commented wryly, 'You'll know this child – he is forever standing on your feet!' And if they have difficulty in accurately gauging the distance between objects, moving round the classroom avoiding tables and chairs can be a real obstacle course.

Any movements which involve turning are difficult for these children because then the cues from the environment are shifting and their points of reference are lost. And balancing along a bench is tricky too, because the children don't appreciate, kinesthetically, where their arms should be held to help them balance.

And even when practised, some children have difficulty in memorising the improved pattern, for

> their kinesthetic memory is impaired out of all proportion to their general intelligence, yet they do not have any gross neurological deficits. (Grimley and McKinley 1977)

This can be very frustrating for the children and their teachers, because progress is not only quite slow, but erratic, and there are days when no progress at all appears to have been made. In fact it can appear as if the children have never heard of the thing they had mastered last time! Considering whether the task size can be reduced, or simply switching off and trying again when the children are less tired, is often the best way.

Directionality

Some children have no conceptual understanding of directions in space – and the space behind their bodies in particular, just doesn't seem to exist! If they don't see it, it's not there! Old-fashioned singing games can be very helpful, e.g. 'Pat-a-Cake, Pat-a-cake Baker's Man' where the children, standing in a circle, beat out a rhythm on the backs of the children in front. This emphasises 'backs' even though they belong to someone else! Or 'In and Out the Dusty Bluebells' where the children have to make accurate spatial decisions if they are to clear the arches made by the children in the circle. Laterality or sidedness does develop quite late in most children: until they are about nine, most will turn and go forwards rather than move in a sideways mode. They need lots of practice to establish forwards and backwards, over, under and through.

Body boundary

Children who have a poor sense of body boundary have difficulty knowing where they end and the outside world begins. They have great difficulty in manipulating bats and pencils and paint brushes, because they do not see them as separate objects. This lack of awareness causes difficulty in controlling the implement, especially if the children have to look up, perhaps to copy from the board. In swimming too, they may bump their heads into the side of the pool because they do not recognise the closing distance between themselves and the pool edge, and so they need lots of head-up, look-ahead, glide-into-the-edge games to keep them safe.

What can be done?

The children need to develop awareness of the relationship between themselves and outside objects and this can be done by 'grasp and let go' activities. The old-fashioned game 'Pin the tail on the donkey' (using blu-tak) is always fun and allows the children to concentrate on the difference between the hand and the tail, and how one lets go! Very young children enjoy putting hoops over spindles and again letting go and seeing the hoop disappear is helpful in gauging the perimeter of the body. Any kind of tactile work will help emphasise body boundary and help the children to make more precise movements – e.g moving balls along an abacus; with older children getting them involved in collage work where cloth or wool has to be stuck down to create a design; placing a large hoop over a standing partner; pushing floats through the water, or any kind of activity where an object has to be held then 'lost'.

Blowing ping-pong balls to the other side of the water tray, all kinds of batting, throwing and kicking help children judge where they end and objects begin. This kind of assessment is critically important in judging distances, a skill which permeates the curriculum, e.g. estimating distances in mathematics, map-reading, setting up circuits, solving problems such as bridge building in environmental studies.

Balance

The most significant ability in movement is balance, because it affects everything children try to do. Recently it has been renamed 'postural control', because that name explains that balance is important in all movements – it is not just the ability to stand on one leg for a few moments. Balance sustains the position of the body in a jump, it steadies the body during a throwing action and it helps body control during changes of direction. Keeping balanced in a forward roll is necessary if the movement is to be controlled and safe – even walking smoothly needs balance. Think back to a toddler newly walking and you'll see what I mean!

There are two different kinds of balance – static balance which is to do with maintaining equilibrium and poise while the body is still, and dynamic balance which comes into play as the body moves. The first would appear to be easier than the second but some young children find it extremely difficult to be still. This may be because they have retained some primary reflexes – the child who can't sit still may be reacting in an involuntary way to the stimulus of his t-shirt rubbing his back! Standing erect and well poised can be difficult if the sense of balance is not adequately developed or if poor muscle tone does not give the joints adequate support. Strangely enough, some children with static balance problems can cope when running – the momentum of that action helping to support their dynamic balance. And so, if adults suspect that the ability to balance is delayed, then assessments for both kinds of balance – both static and dynamic – have to be made.

What can be done?
Vision helps considerably in maintaining balance and if children are experiencing difficulties then helping them to fix their gaze, perhaps on a picture on the wall, can help give them a stable point of reference. Mirrors tend to confuse the children because of giving 'back to front' cues. Children need time to be steady, to look and fix their point of reference, to feel the correct alignment and possibly they need to be supported to give confidence in the first tries. The children themselves should be allowed to repeat an activity until they indicate that they are ready to move on. The 'move' may mean changing the skill or the environment, but probably not both at the same time!

Coordination

> Coordination is the ability to control independent body parts involved in a complex movement pattern and to integrate these parts in a single smooth successful effort at achieving some goal. (Singer 1973)

As different movements involve many different parts or just a few, the kind of coordination which needs to be used to achieve efficient movement varies too.

The skill itself may primarily require eye–foot coordination as in kicking a ball; hand–eye coordination as in throwing a beanbag into a pail; and/or whole-body coordination as in running and jumping, when all parts of the body are involved in completing a task. The kind of coordination required differs according to which body parts are used, the sequencing they require and the time pattern that is employed. Skill in one kind does not necessarily imply total command, so challenges involving a range of coordinations need to be assessed.

Children with coordination difficulties have problems in synchronising their movements so that they can appear 'all fingers and thumbs', clutching at air as the ball sails past, having to stop walking or running before they place the dish on the table, or not being able to move out of the way as they close the door. They can't do two types of task at the same time. The children don't easily 'get it together' and tend to have stilted rather than flowing movement patterns. 'Awkward' and 'jerky' are common descriptors of the way children with coordination difficulties move.

What can be done?

Adults need to visualise then analyse the separate components of the ideal pattern then compare that to the children's demonstration. The next thing is to reduce the task demand, and gradually build up the original pattern. If, for example, the children can't kick a moving ball because they overrun and mistime the action so that they perhaps just scuff the top of the ball, then they should practise kicking a stationary ball to help timing, then a slow moving ball (the child stationary, the ball fed sympathetically to the kicking foot), then kicking a moving ball. These are all practices which need to be accomplished before any partner work or involvement in a larger game can be enjoyed.

Rhythm

Every movement has a preparation, then an action, then a recovery phase and when these blend together in sequential movements, a rhythm emerges. The motor control needed to sustain the rhythm will be very different depending on whether gross or fine movements are involved. This is why some children who can play the piano, showing good fine motor rhythm, find difficulty in gross motor skills, e.g. in running and taking off into a jump at the correct time. They may dither, and the flow of the action is spoiled. Usually a break in the rhythm means that the action is inefficient, and this is why having the children listen to the rhythm is an important teaching aid. The rhythm of a shuttlecock on a wooden bat can help them in timing the next stroke and in judging the amount of strength required to maintain the flight pattern, but they must be able to listen.

Teachers usually associate rhythm with dance type movements and this is a good medium for understanding two different kinds of rhythm. The first kind of rhythm would emanate from the child's movement and this would be the most usual in the nursery. Asking children to move to an outside rhythm, i.e. one imposed by music or poetry, is much more difficult for in this kind of activity the children have to adapt their natural movement rhythm to 'fit' the music. Having said that, some children are spot on in intricate Scottish or even Irish dances where they must move incredibly quickly if they are to sustain the rhythm, so again the teaching must be appropriate for the skill level of each child. Most children with dyspraxia would find this kind of challenge too great but I have seen one very determined ten-year-old girl, who had had a diagnosis of dyspraxia confirmed, practise and practise the steps until they were at the correct tempo. It's amazing what motivation can achieve!

Each child has an inherent repertoire of movement abilities which change due to maturation, experience and development and, as noted above, perseverance. And so it is vital that the individual profile of each child with difficulties is compiled and monitored and an individual programme of remediation developed to help. Children who don't need specific help won't be harmed by joining in, but children with difficulties will be held back, even damaged, if their individual needs are not met.

Speed of movement

Parents and teachers in the research group were often concerned that their children were 'too slow'. What did they mean? They explained that while some 'couldn't get started, but once they were going they were fine', others were 'generally slow-paced' or 'began alright and then were distracted by something else in the vicinity and their performance faded away'.

They were interested to find that there were two different kinds of difficulty inherent in response time. The first is reaction time. This is the term used to describe the time elapsing between the perception of a stimulus and the beginning of the reaction to it. Children with quick reaction time do well in competitive activities of short duration such as sprinting, or in games where instructions are called out and the children are required to make an immediate response. (This should not be confused with reflex action which is automatic.)

Movement time is the time taken by the movement itself, while the term 'response time' covers both reaction and movement time. Improving reaction time takes lots of practice of the 'ready, steady, go' kind, while improving the movement time requires analysis of the movement pattern into its preparation, action and recovery phases so that appropriate help can be given.

If children are having difficulties, then this level of analysis, i.e. of the activity and the necessary underlying abilities, is needed to find the true area which needs to be helped.

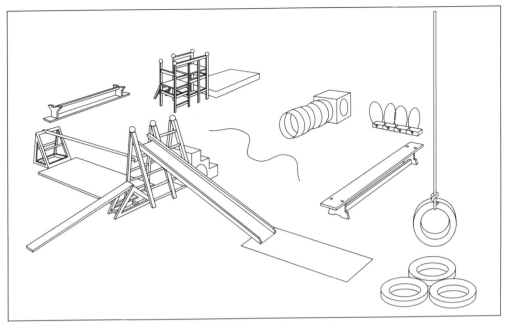

Figure 5.2 Large apparatus layout for outdoor play

Outdoor play on large apparatus

Let's go back now and revisit some of the children who were playing outside on the large apparatus, arranged as in Figure 5.2.

The apparatus was arranged:

- to allow the children to demonstrate their ability in the basic movement patterns, i.e. walking, running, crawling, climbing and swinging
- to allow teachers and nursery nurses to observe perceptual abilities and movement abilities (see Table 5.1).

NB The distance between each piece was carefully planned so that the children had time to recover from a 'fast' move before they tackled balancing, and so that any uncontrolled landing would not interfere, possibly dangerously, with other activities.

The children generally chose what they wanted to do and in which order. This is why all safety possibilities had to be considered in the layout plan. However, for the purposes of observation we encouraged the children to follow a circuit so that all the basic skills and competences could be caught on video. This is because recording very detailed observations over several activities provides objective evidence for discussion and a sound basis for planning the most relevant kind of help.

Table 5.1 Apparatus and skills/competences to be observed

Apparatus	Skills/competences to be observed
(a) Broad benches for easy balancing	Confident walking; change of direction
(b) Tyre on rope for swinging	Strong arms pulling the body upright
(c) Wiggly worm; S-shaped rope	Control in moving on a curved path
(d) Wooden box and plastic barrel	Crawling, showing arm strength to pull out of the barrel
(e) Balancing bench, narrow side up	Balancing, poise, control
(f) Climbing, crawling, jumping, landing	Each skill separately and control in transitions
(g) Mattress for safe landing	Resilience in landing; control and ability to move on
(h) Hoops for crawling through	Body awareness of feet; 'out of sight' control

The arrangement of large apparatus is very important for all children, but even more so for children with movement difficulties because they need more time and more space to reorientate after jumping down, or turning, or clambering through barrels. Careful planning of the apparatus layout can ensure that e.g. sliding down a chute is followed by hoops on the ground which can be bowled into an open space. This kind of arrangement gives children time to catch their breath and cope.

Teachers need to visualise all the movement responses which children might make and consider the recovery time of the least able child. Difficult equipment should therefore be interspersed with less demanding apparatus. After all, children who do not need time to reorientate can avoid the easy bits or just move faster. Whenever there are children with movement difficulties – and there almost always are – then there has to be room for falling!

Remember **Tom**, the child described on p. 19? He is the well-built child who tends to barge – he goes too fast and can never stop in time. He has chosen to try to balance along the narrow side of a low bench.

Analysis

1. Visualising the correct way – the teacher's preparation!
2. Observing and recording Tom's way
3. Helping Tom

Visualising the 'ideal' helps observers compare the child's performance to that picture and gives pointers to where help is required.

1. Visualisation

Preparation: Moving forward carefully and getting upright on the bench.

Transition 1: Adjusting the weight on to the back foot ready to move forward, and holding balance possibly by pressing the free foot against the beam.

Action: Walking smoothly forward, poised and balanced, at the correct speed, without too much looking down at the bench, arms held out if necessary to help balance.

Transition 2: Judging the distance to the end of the bench, altering the stride pattern so that the back foot is at the edge, bringing the free foot through and using the momentum of the swing to lead into a jump off.

Recovery: Landing, in control, knees bent to absorb the momentum and retaining enough power to bring the body up to standing, ready to move on.

2. Observing and recording Tom's way

Preparation: Tom lumbered up to the bench, using big strides, arms swinging across his body. He stopped abruptly at the edge, his feet too near and this caused him to flop over to grip the bench. He pushed himself up then began to get on. To do this he leant well forward over the bench and his weight was over his right push-up leg. In this semi-crouched position he had to use too much strength to push his trunk erect. Being too close to the bench, he had no momentum from the approach to help. This meant that a strong push was necessary and as a result he was off balance as he began his walk.

Transition 1: Tom tried to adjust his balance, controlling the strength from the exaggerated push-up. He stood with all his weight on his right foot and swung his arms wildly to try to find the point of balance.

Action: Tom then tried to control the momentum of the arm swaying action by thumping his feet hard on each stride along the bench. This made the bench wobble so Tom moved even faster.

Transition 2: He tried to anticipate the jump off, but not being able to slow down he more or less flopped off the bench.

Photo 8 Tom

Recovery. Tom landed heavily with a deep knee bend and collapsed on to the ground.

Comment. Tom thought this was great fun. He had enjoyed being nearly out of control, and having the hard feedback from his thumping step pattern. Would he have the patience to learn to do it properly? Because Tom was heavily built with muscular thighs, he needed a swaying action to make one pass the other. This caused overbalancing and the movement being almost out of control.

3. Helping Tom
Tom needed to rethink the preparatory phase first – or else he would never move on to balancing on the narrow side of the bench. Standing at the edge rather than moving into the action was helpful. He then had to push his head high and feel the balanced position before progressing. He also had to pass one leg close to the other as swinging it out was knocking him off balance.

Practices

(a) Facing the teacher across the bench with Tom standing about a foot away. The teacher should stand close to the bench with arms held towards the child so that he is not tempted to lean far forward to grab support. He should place his chosen foot flat on to the bench and push up to hold and feel the poised position. Once this has been done, a beanbag balanced on the head gives the child something to push against and adds challenge, because if the bag falls off then the push up hasn't been straight.

(b) Once getting on in a controlled way has been achieved, the walk along needs to sustain this slower, quieter action. Asking the child to estimate and then count the steps to the end of the bench (or two benches lined up end to end so that the activity appears more difficult, not just a 'boring' practice!) helps concentration and slows the action. Asking the child to listen – 'don't make the bench wobble, keep it silent' – also helps the child to be focused.

(c) Once the walk is controlled, the jump off is much easier. Tom still needs to control his feet, however, and keep facing forward rather than twisting the body to the side. Giving into the landing and springing up out of the ground can be helped by the teacher calling out the rhythm.

Comment

Balance is important at all stages, even in the jump off. This can only be achieved by getting Tom to go more slowly. This is not easy because he enjoys the swaying, lumbering action. So he needs some kind of challenge to compensate. Having a broad side bench followed by a narrow side up gives two levels, and adding the beanbag on the head helps body awareness and body boundary, i.e. feeling the top of the head immediately over the feet, and so aiding balancing.

Now **Ben**. He is the child who has floppy arms and poor upper body strength. He was described on p. 20.

Ben is crawling through a wooden box and then into a plastic barrel. He normally avoids any action that requires him to put his weight on his arms, however he is intrigued by the layout of the apparatus and wants to follow his friends in a follow-my-leader game.

1. Visualisation
Preparation: Moving forward and crouching down ready to move into the box.

Transition 1: Bending forward into prone kneeling, ready for the crawling action.

Action: Crawling through the box, into and through the barrel. Correct crawling action.

Transition 2: Holding the arms firmly to support the body weight as the feet get ready to take over. Fingers spread wide to help balance.

Recovery: Weight is transferred on to the feet, the body straightens up and the walking away is resumed.

2. Observing and recording Ben's way
Preparation: No difficulties here. Ben approached the task eagerly but without undue haste. He placed his hands inside the box, but without any obvious weight bearing, and pushed strongly with his legs to begin.

Transition 1: Close observation here found that Ben was keeping almost all his weight on his knees, and shuffling through the box. His hands were lightly touching the grass but there was no sign of weight bearing or propulsion. His trunk was as upright as it could be in such a confined space.

Action: The shuffling action appeared to continue through the barrel, although it was difficult to see inside.

Transition 2: Gathering the body weight to come out of the barrel was causing Ben to grimace, showing his difficulty in using his arms effectively.

Photo 9 Ben

Recovery: As Ben had not sufficient strength in his arms, he put the top of his head on the ground and used that to lever his hips through the tunnel. He then tried to follow his friends on to the next piece of apparatus, but as his weight had not been transferred back over to his feet sufficiently to support him (faulty transition), trying to stand from that position caused him to fall over towards the wooden box. He tried to put out his hands to save himself, but his arms, being weak, gave minimal protection, merely shielding his face. His head and shoulders crashed into the box.

Comment: This was the first time that Ben's lack of arm strength had caused him to be hurt and the staff were very upset. They decided to ask for immediate physiotherapy input as they had not the specialist knowledge, equipment or enough time for the kind of concentrated individual help they anticipated would be necessary. In the meantime, they were going to reconsider the layout of apparatus so that Ben's enthusiasm and lack of control would not lead him into danger.

3. Helping Ben

Ben's parents immediately took him to their GP who contacted a physiotherapy unit and a programme of strengthening exercises was established. Ben was a first child and a much longed for child and initially the parents were very upset that their bright boy

Photo 10 Ben

Photo 11 Ben

had a difficulty. They had noticed that he was 'ambidextrous', not realising that in changing his pencil from one hand to the other to complete e.g. drawing a circle, he in fact had mixed dominance and was unable to complete tasks which meant crossing the midline. This was one instance where outdoor gross motor skill difficulties caused parents, teachers and nursery nurses to reflect together on these and on fine motor skills used indoors, e.g. cutting at snack time, colouring-in, and they discovered that the total picture was that of a child needing immediate help.

His parents volunteered that possibly they had treated Ben younger than his chronological age would suggest, e.g. helping him to dress, cutting his food for him and generally doing too much. They explained that they had waited so long for this child and enjoyed doing all they could for him. The teachers were able to explain that this would not have caused Ben's difficulty, but may possibly have disguised the problem. However, it had been identified now and help was at hand. They also emphasised how bright the child was and how sociable and this prevented any feelings of guilt or inadequacy. After their initial disappointment, they were relieved that the difficulty had been picked up and they were approaching the physiotherapy positively. They also intended to pull back at home so that Ben could have practice in the everyday coping skills and become more independent.

Now **Ian**, the child described on p. 22. Ian stumbled and tripped, gently, and made no fuss. He followed Ben around quite closely and appeared to copy whatever he did. In this observation he had chosen to crawl through a set of widely spaced coloured hoops which were supported on plastic bricks, about 15cm from the ground. After this he climbed up on to a wooden box, ready to jump off.

1. Visualisation
Preparation: Walking towards the apparatus and stooping down at the correct distance from the opening to place the hands along the bricks; knees should be firmly supporting the weight and toes should be curled under, ready to hoist the weight on to the hands.

Transition 1: The weight should be transferred on to the arms and hands, ready for the legs and feet to enter the hoops.

Action: The crawling action should be coordinated with the limbs held tightly together so that the legs and feet stay inside the hoops.

Transition 2: The arms leading the body out of the hoops should be strong enough to take the whole body weight, allowing the lower body to pull out of the hoops.

Action: The weight needs to be transferred back to the feet to allow the arms to move on to the climbing box.

2. Observing and recording Ian's way
Preparation: Ian began competently, judging the distance accurately and stooping down to go into the hoop, only slightly knocking the hoops with his head. He seemed unaware of this, even though the hoops shook a bit.

Transition 1: His arms were strongly supporting his weight, but his legs were making no contribution. They were really just lying behind his strong upper half – the toes were not curled under, ready to push.

Action: Ian pulled forward into a crawling position with minimal help from his feet and legs. His arms moved forwards strongly, but he couldn't keep his feet within the hoops. Furthermore, as he was looking forwards he couldn't retrieve his feet and pull them back in line. He had to look round to see where his feet were, then he pulled them in, upsetting the hoops which had to be replaced by a helpful little girl.

Photo 12 Ian

Transition 2: Pulling out of the hoops again depended on strong arms. His hips were raised very high, and as a result he tipped forward. His strong arms met the climbing box and he pulled up on to that strongly, again trailing his legs.

Comment: Ian has two problems. The first is the lack of strength in his legs, the second is poor body awareness in the lower half of his body.

3. Helping Ian
A programme of activities was developed and all the children who wanted to join in did so. They enjoyed games like 'Angels in the Snow' and 'Simon Says' to develop body awareness, and strengthening leg exercises. These were all done in a group and the other children didn't realise that they were especially designed to help Ian.

The staff considered that although Ian should go on to Primary 1 according to his birth date, his general level of maturation would make it advisable for him to have another year in nursery. The parents considered that this would be helpful and that the activity programme should be continued and carefully monitored to see if that input plus maturation would be enough to overcome his difficulties. If there was not enough progress quite soon, then applying for physiotherapy was to be considered.

The three children given as examples were in groups of thirty in an 'ordinary' nursery. There were several others who had a range of difficulties. The staff who had participated found recording the detailed observations very time-consuming but as a result they realised that their discussions about the children, based on 'evidence', had become less general and pointed to particular kinds of help. They were also surprised to find that they didn't always 'see the same things', although this tended to be in the detail. There was no disagreement in identifying the children who had problems.

The staff found that the observations contributed greatly to their baseline assessment records. The records were welcomed by the receiving primary schools as they now had pointers for developing their own physical education programme and for making changes to the classroom organisation and routine.

CHAPTER 6

Social and psychological difficulties

The self-concept, giving praise and understanding friendships

Although the first 'telling' signs of difficulties may be in moving, the as-difficult or more difficult, possibly even more enduring problems are to do with the children's self-concept, i.e. the picture they build of themselves, and within that their self-esteem, i.e. how much they value that picture, because these have a profound effect on how they approach new activities, new friendships, indeed learning itself.

The self-concept is based on a reciprocal analysis. Children build a picture of themselves in terms of how they think others perceive them, i.e. 'What I think of myself depends on what I think you think of me!' This has been called a 'tri-dimensional image', a name which shows the complexity of the concept, but doesn't really explain how it is formed! James (cited in Gallahue 1993) tries to do this by explaining that when two people meet, there are really six people present – each person as he or she is, each as the other sees him or her and each as seen by him or herself, and all these 'people' are influential in forming the self-concept, which is really an amalgam of their evaluations. Cooley (1962) called this 'the looking-glass self', a name which highlights the reflection involved in building the picture.

Two other variables are important. First, the resilience of the children themselves, and resilience <———> vulnerability can be found at opposite ends of one continuum describing an important personality trait. The children's position on this will help to determine how they are affected by their interpretation of the judgments of others – the most resilient children being able to shrug off the negative vibes which would devastate the most vulnerable.

The second is to do with the esteem the children give to those making the judgments – those they see as being important having a greater influence. And so parents, teachers, nursery nurses and popular children are likely to be significant in the children's self-evaluations. Even then, the children's perception is not fixed. At first parents are the most critical influences in the children's environment and then teachers appear to take over. Everyone knows the feeling when 'Miss so-and-so says' dominates the day. Usually this change comes around age five or six, so it primarily affects children in the early years. And if parents and teachers have different ideas and standards, or at least if the children assert that they have, then there can be confusion, even trouble!

One little boy, Calum, had his dad, Jim, for his teacher. He seemed to believe that they were two separate people. At home his dad was bemused when Calum explained his day at school as if his dad had not been there – 'Guess what, Dad, we did cooking today!' – and he was irritated when Calum played one off against the other – 'No, that's not the way to do it, Mr Thomas says it's better to do it this way . . .' when Jim was sure he'd said no such thing! Perhaps Calum needed two distinct role models, perhaps he needed to separate home and school experiences in his mind or perhaps building and sustaining two kinds of relationships with the same person – the one at school being slightly more formal – was confusing. Certainly, understanding children and the influences which affect their self-concept isn't always easy!

This kind of scenario brings home the importance of understanding children's perception of events. If they are secure, confident youngsters they are more likely to dwell on the good things that happened in the day. If, however, they are vulnerable and unsure, they are more likely to dwell on real or imagined hurts. This is why two children can 'honestly' give very different accounts of the same incident.

Later, the peer group become the most important influence on the children. This is when children want to dress the same and 'have to have' or 'be allowed to do' whatever is in vogue! Is this creeping down into the early years?

And so the children's picture of themselves is their self-concept and part of that is their self-esteem (see Figure 6.1). This is a kind of evaluation where the children compare the model they have of themselves to their ideal, i.e. what they would like to be! The

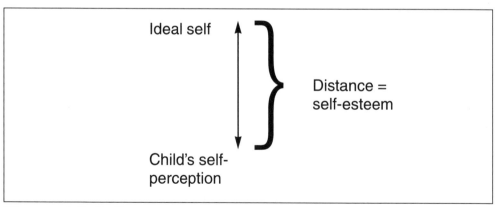

Figure 6.1 Self-esteem

children are likely to have two sets of comparisons – the first in the unrealistic category e.g. pop idols or top level sports men and women, and while they may imitate, they know that aspirations to be just like them are not realistic or immediately attainable. But much nearer to home are the other children, the peer group who have all the desirable attributes, in the view of the evaluating children. The distance between the children's evaluations of themselves in relation to these others is the prime factor in the formation of the self-esteem.

In earlier research, Macintyre (1997) asked children aged five about the things they would best like to be able to do well. Apart from one or two wild cards – 'I'd like to fly' – most children spoke of being a ballet dancer or a footballer or a motor cyclist, i.e. 'movement things', and when they were asked 'Do you know someone who can do that?' they gave the names of someone in their immediate group, not high-level performers. This showed that people around them were their role models. Interestingly some children estimated that with practice they would be able to do it too, while others decided that the skills required were beyond them and they wouldn't like to try. And so the children's self-esteem was either encouraging or preventing them from practising.

But how do young children come to make these judgments? From their earliest days they are surrounded by adult talk, e.g. 'Isn't he a big boy?' when the child, from the tone of voice, realises he's not and wishes he was, or 'We've taken the stabilisers off Liam's bike', making the rider feel that he, too, should be coping without. Gradually, absorbing these kinds of comments begins to affect the self-esteem, at first in a vague kind of way, but as nursery days pass, these comments and attitudes have a longer-lasting effect.

An important component of self-esteem is body image, i.e. how the children perceive their own bodies and how near that picture matches the 'ideal', usually the slim, strong, 'cool' model child. Even in the early years, children are surrounded by such images and they can be severely affected by their self-perceived lack of worth, because young children tend to stay with surface qualities.

Listen to Christopher telling us about himself and then a friend.

I am Christopher. I am very big and I am six and a lot. I have red hair and I can't go out in the sun too much. I have new shoes and I like Star Wars, and I don't have a cat now.

My friend is Peter but he's not as big as me and he is seven. (Long pause.) He's always cross but sometimes he's funny and he's a bit fat. He has fair hair and he's pudgy and he can't run as fast as me.

Christopher obviously likes being big and feels a little superior in that his friend is 'a bit fat'. His immediate judgments are about how his friend looks. He doesn't really focus on abilities, but when he does, it's movement that springs to mind. Older children focus much more on deeper qualities like kindness and reliability and are less likely to talk about appearance factors, although the amount of time spent on self-care and in despairing over 'spots and size' proves that they are still important.

Harter (1990) claims that it is inappropriate to say that preschool children have a high or low self-esteem. This is because they have only made self-evaluations on a number of separate skills. By six or seven, rarely earlier, she says, the children combine the judgments about themselves into a global self-esteem and this is harder to change. Bee (1998) suggests that the greater cognitive skill which comes about at age seven, partly due to schooling, partly due to acquiring maturational skills such as conservation, contributes to the development of global self-worth, and that the children's overall assessment of themselves influences both their motivation and their willingness, even their capacity to form relationships.

Much recent research focuses on children building a mental model of 'who I am'. Bretherton (1991) explains that this mental model is the result of experiences the children have had, and that it 'shapes the kind of experiences they seek'. It can be seen, therefore, how important the quality of the early years is, for the judgments the children make about themselves are going to influence how they confront all the new experiences they will have at home and in school.

There, all sorts of 'doing things' are highly valued by children and of course they are immediately open to public assessment. For while poor writing skills and wrong answers can be hidden in jotters, and later sympathetic, individual help can be given, 'not being able to run and forward roll, or catch a ball' is easily spotted by sometimes scathing peers. Is it any wonder children who have coordination difficulties don't want to try?

Russell (1988) claims that

> Repeated failure in front of their peers to match normal performance of skills in the lesson, produces and gradually hardens an attitude of failure. They can't play, nobody wants to dance with them; they are never chosen or are last to be chosen for teams; classmates laugh at their inability to cope. This situation reinforces their feelings of inadequacy and their self-esteem and self-image are destroyed.

To add to their frustrations, Sherril (1993) explains that children who stay at the lower performance level, i.e. those who move at the initial or elementary level for longer than their peers,

> have inefficient and energy exhausting movement patterns which affect their social acceptance and their self-esteem.

The movement patterns are exhausting because they are non-habitual and because constant whole-body movements are used. And the children, doubting that they can be successful, are likely to be worried and tense, further mitigating against their success. Think back to learning to drive or ski or using a computer. Remember how it felt?

A strong influence on the stability of the self-esteem is the amount and consistency of support the children have from the people around them. If the children consider that they are liked as they are, then they are likely to be confident and have a high self-esteem. However, this does not hold if they feel that they are not meeting the standards which they have set for themselves. The most stressful situation arises if the children consider that the support they receive is contingent on their doing well, that liking is somehow part of a bargain. Devastating, too, is the scenario when the parents pressurise their children towards achieving unrealistic goals which can only result in 'failure'. So what can be done?

The importance of praise

The main aim is to give children confidence in their own abilities, therefore they must have success and realise that pleasure in their progress, rather than in their attainment, is shared by people who are important to them, i.e. their significant others. And so they need opportunities where they can be praised. Very young children are likely to respond to unrealistic praise and this can be effective and provide time for some skills to be gained. However for the slightly older, more discerning children, this may only heighten their feelings of inadequacy. It is best if children can have genuine praise for identifiable progress so that they can feel a real sense of achievement.

Margaret Pope (1988), a head teacher of children with learning difficulties, writes:

> I have been amazed at how well a child responds to an acceptance of his or her difficulties when this is coupled with positive activities that can lead to improvements. Telling a child he is good at something, when as an intelligent human being he knows he's not, far from raising his self-esteem only reduces it.

Tasks, then, have to be real challenges scaled down to permit achievement. This involves reducing the demands of the task and/or the environment and possibly praising quietly when other children are not able to claim or demonstrate that they can do it better! Giving extra physical support when the children have difficulties can also help, although they should not be attempting movements on large apparatus which are well beyond their capabilities, i.e. where they have to cling on!

Children with low self-esteem are likely to deny that they have made progress. 'That was luck', they'll say, rather than 'I did it better', or 'Those sums were easier today', rather than 'I got them right!' They have difficulty in acknowledging that they have made any kind of progress. Children with dyspraxia especially need to have any improvement clearly spelled out for them, because teachers can't take it for granted that the children will recognise it for themselves.

An interesting piece of research by Felker (Gurney 1987) which looked into ways of raising self-esteem gave two pieces of advice. The first: 'Teachers, praise yourselves'; the second: 'Teach the children to praise themselves and others.' Unfortunately, the research which was carried out in secondary schools couldn't give appropriate advice to nurseries and infant classrooms, but one strategy which we tried as a result of discussing the idea was for the teacher, at the end of the day, to summarise the new learning which had been covered, perhaps only highlighting two or three key points. The teachers in this research found that they were often surprised by the number of new things they had achieved and they claimed that doing this, i.e. making an end-of-day summary, fostered a sense of pride in both themselves and the children. An added bonus was that the children going out of school would sometimes have a real answer when their parents asked, 'What did you do in school today?' And so both the teacher and the pupils went home feeling good. This gave a positive end to the day and also reinforced some teaching points!

But what about the second piece of advice? How were the children going to learn to praise themselves and compliment the other children?

In the primaries, the teachers began to look at the possibility of introducing self-assessment. They found that they could only do this with one or two children each day and they wondered whether the time taken was worth it when the children did not have a great deal of knowledge to make such assessments. What they did discover, however, was that sometimes the children used different assessment criteria from themselves. When they talked with the children about their story writing, they found that the children most often thought the teacher wanted them to be neat, rather than having interesting ideas or following a storyline structure. This led to some teachers realising that they had not reinforced their own criteria enough, and others wondering how the children had stayed with the neatness idea, when they had explained several times that in the first rough draft, neatness was not an issue! In one or two cases the teachers abandoned their criteria and moved towards the children's choice because 'that gives us a better idea of the things that are important to them'. Once these had been achieved, the teachers' own criteria were used as extension work.

When they tried to have the children praise each other, they found that generally speaking the children stayed with surface judgments just as Christopher had done. They spoke of 'having a pretty dress or liking someone's hair', not exactly profound thoughts, and very often they did not mention the children who needed praise. This was disappointing; however, the idea was taken forward in 'Circle Time' when each child in turn had a special day.

The drive reduction theory

Strangely enough, although we tend to assume that success is motivating, continuous success can be self-defeating. If success follows success too often, the challenge and therefore the interest is lost. On the other hand it is not surprising that for 99.9 per cent of children, constant negative feedback also leads to abandoning the activity. This is why intermittent positive and negative feedback appears to be the recipe for ongoing motivation.

Child (1986) calls this the drive reduction theory (see Figure 6.2). Perhaps this explains why a playground game like skipping is all the rage then suddenly it's abandoned, i.e. when the skill challenge has been consistently met, or why, for some adults, golf is endlessly intriguing, because it is extremely hard to sustain successful play all the way round a golf course!

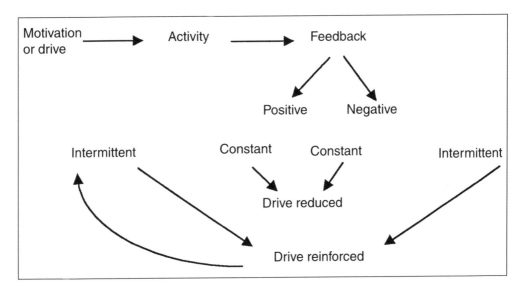

Figure 6.2 The drive reduction theory

This feedback from the activity itself is a little different from the verbal feedback given to the children by others, although the idea of intermittency still holds true. Praise is most beneficial when it is used as positive feedback which contains teaching points – why the action was good and what the child needs to do next. Praise alone, e.g. 'Good, go on, I know you can do it', isn't much help when the child really doesn't know what 'doing it' involves.

Even less productive of course is negative feedback, but no-one dealing with children would give that, unless it was unintentional and was communicated through non-verbals. If the voice says 'Well done', but the body language does not agree, possibly showing tension and communicating disquiet, or – when the child has regressed – despair, the negative message is likely to be the one which is retained. And so all of those who want to praise have to be careful that their verbals and non-verbals agree. If they don't, metaincongruence results and the children are confused by receiving contrasting signals. Argyle (1969) claims that 90 per cent of the meaning within communication comes through the non-verbals. If this is so, then body language needs as much care as oral, otherwise the benefits of praising are going to be lost.

Praise which is given frequently but not too often and based on the assessment of a genuine effort will make an important contribution to raising the children's self-esteem. This is especially important for the vulnerable children, the worriers, who are sure they will 'never be able to do it well'.

The importance of practice

Hopefully, praise will encourage children to practise and hopefully this will prove to be beneficial in helping the acquisition of skill. If children are going to practise willingly, then the activities have to be fun and those that have been suggested throughout this text have been tried and tested!

Having said that, it can be difficult to persuade children to practise skills that pose problems as they probably don't realise how important rehearsal/practice is. Only with practice will skills become habitual and give a sound foundation for superimposing other movements.

Happily, being very good at just one or two activities seems to compensate for finding a battery of others difficult, and keeps the self-esteem high. This is more likely if the successful activities are valued by the 'significant others'.

For children who find balancing difficult, that is when riding a bicycle or skating is out of the question, being able to swim offers a huge compensation. For the speed swimmer a good sense of balance is vital, but for the beginner the water will support and all the limbs can be used to aid floating, the basis of all swimming strokes. The children can have fun with the others as they get to grips with the coordination of different strokes.

Above all the children must feel they are making progress. Then they will be prepared to practise until they can say, ' Look at me, I can do it too.'

Friendships

An important contributor to the children's self-esteem is whether they have friends. Friendships can be categorised as either vertical or horizontal, and Hartup (1989) suggests that children need to experience both kinds. Vertical relationships are those that children form with older people, e.g. parents, teachers, even older brothers and sisters, i.e. those who have more knowledge and experience. That kind of relationship, although possibly very strong, is one of giving and receiving and the source of attachment for the children and affectational bonds for the parents.

In horizontal friendships, however, those involved, e.g. children at play, have equal social powers and similar amounts of knowledge and experience and so egalitarian relationships can be formed. Vertical friendships give the children security and nurture, and within these they learn the values, attitudes and social norms of their cultural group. Horizontal friendships allow children to practise these learned patterns, and through sharing ideas, discussing and arguing with their peers, they begin to rationalise and form their own value systems. And as the children make more friends and gain different experiences this continues and explains, at least in part, the adolescent battles which may occur when young people reject some or all of the family's standards. But how and when do these horizontal friendships begin?

Children begin to be interested in other children as early as six months of age, poking eyes, pulling hair, in fact investigating them as objects. But this is usually curtailed and toys are preferred as they jingle or do other interesting things. At 14 months or so, children play side by side, aware of each other but only occasionally cooperating. They have moved from solitary play to parallel play.

Around 18 months, toddlers begin to show 'playmate preferences', and these can be surprisingly enduring, but the interaction is quite basic. The children play near one another, seemingly secure in each other's company, but still they do their own thing. A grass roots change is obvious around three to four years when children prefer to play together and cooperation and meaningful interaction take place.

There is some evidence that children are consistent in seeking out the same playmate at this play-group/nursery age, when children are beginning to realise that they can leave their parents or carers and they will be sure to return. However, for some children, parting can be traumatic and they may regress to an earlier form of coping, or not coping. Accurate observations of children's friendship patterns need to wait until the children are freed from this kind of concern, or biased data will result.

At four years, group play begins, very often 'pretend play already organised around gender lines' (Hartup 1989). Perhaps the kind of play determines the composition of the group: thinking of 'firemen' and 'weddings' as possible topics, this would appear to be a reasonable explanation. Gottman (1986) claims that most early friendships in the preschool years, 65 per cent in fact, are same sex. The picture at school age is even more segregated, as by then, friendship pairs are almost exclusively of the same sex.

But why should this be? Maccoby (1990) offers one clue. In her study of friendships, she showed that boys and girls had very different modes of interaction. The girls used an 'enabling' style which was characterised by partners supporting each other, agreeing and making suggestions, whereas boys generally demonstrated a 'constricting' style. She explained that this, in contrast to the girls' more conciliatory way, tended to 'derail' any interaction, thus bringing it to an end. The characteristic features of the boys' conversations were 'contradicting, boasting and other forms of self-display'. While girls made requests, e.g. 'Can I have a turn?', boys demanded, 'Give me that!'

If this is so, it could explain why girls avoid boys' interactions and bond together and why some boys, possibly the less confident, avoid such confrontation. And as most children with dyspraxia are boys, this finding could go some way to explaining why many prefer to play alone.

But why should some children be helpful and others harmful? To understand we need to look at the development of the characteristics which underline these traits.

Altruism and aggression

At either end of a continuum of social behaviours are altruism at the positive pole and aggression at the negative. Altruism or pro-social behaviour first appears at age two or three, when children in a real sense begin to play with others. At this developmental stage they can empathise with children who are upset or hurt because they have the experience to know how it feels. They have also, as the recipients of bumps and bruises, been surrounded by role models who have shown how to cope and care. Youngsters with dyspraxia, however, seem not to be able to empathise with children or carers, and so they do not offer comfort in a way that creates a friendship bond. And so they lose out on the opportunity to make a friend and possibly are resented, even rejected, because they seem aloof, making no move to help.

Another symptom of dyspraxia mitigates against their making friends. This is the difficulty they have in following 'rules'. Taking turns, sharing toys, waiting and listening to another child's news, these are important in establishing order and security in groups of children. Moreover, the novelty of having rules makes them interesting, and breaking them is easily spotted. In addition, dyspraxic children tend to be impulsive, acting with no appreciation of the consequences. If these actions disrupt others and/or break the classroom rules, and then the 'guilty' show no remorse – and how can they, because they don't realise they have transgressed what are, after all, unwritten rules – as a result, they are labelled as 'naughty children' and those who prefer to conform will not choose them as friends.

How are other children likely to react?

While young children do often support their new friends and show helpful altruistic behaviours, they also tease, argue and fight, i.e. they use aggressive behaviours. However these change as children mature. Children of two or three years will hit out if thwarted, i.e. they use physical aggression, but as their verbal skills improve they use taunts or name-calling instead. The exception to this is in boy pairs, at least American boy pairs, who stay physically aggressive for much longer (Offord *et al.* 1991; see Table 6.1).

Do boys and girls react in the same way?

The area of aggression/competitiveness/dominance is one which is consistent with gender stereotypes, as boys do show more of these types of behaviours throughout junior school. Interestingly, boys also tend to gather in larger groups and are more likely to engage in sports or other common activities. And when they play outside, they move around further from home than girls do. None of these attributes is likely to appeal to children with dyspraxia or help them to make friends.

Table 6.1 Percentage of boys and girls aged 4–11 rated by their teachers as displaying each type of aggressive behaviour

Behaviour	Boys	Girls
Mean to others	21.8	9.6
Physically attacks people	18.1	4.4
Gets in many fights	30.9	9.8
Destroys own things	10.7	2.1
Destroys others' things	10.6	4.4
Threatens to hurt people	13.1	4.0

Source: Offord *et al.* 1991.

It goes without saying that children on the receiving end of aggression or who are not allowed to play suffer greatly as do their parents. Listen to Iona, Paul's mother.

My whole day revolves around worrying whether Paul will manage to get someone to play. What can you say to a wee boy who asks why no-one will play with him? I tried giving him packs of sweets to distribute to all the children for I had tried to explain about sharing, and this helped for the one day, but it didn't last. He couldn't seem to join in. In his first year at nursery there wasn't a problem, but after that the children seemed to go into groups and Paul felt very rejected. If this is the fate of children with difficulties, what are we to do?

Given all this information, would the most helpful thing be for boys with dyspraxia to play with girls in the hope that they would meet with more understanding, or would this line up more difficulties, perhaps in their being distressed by realising that they are not doing what other boys do? Is it true that boys and girls are so intrinsically different?

Gender: the development of gender schema

Martin (1991) explains the development of gender schema. He claims that this begins to develop as soon as children can consistently differentiate between boys and girls. Then, once the children realise their own sex, most are highly motivated to adopt the social conventions which surround it. In early years' schooling, teachers have taken many steps to avoid gender bias, e.g. having a picture of a motor bike by a girl's coat peg and being sure that stories or later reading books do not reinforce sex stereotypes, but still, even at play, sex-role differences emerge as boys choose construction toys and girls go straight for the house corner.

New entrants observe other children and learn from their example, and of course in many homes parents reinforce the boy/girl stereotyping by the toys they buy, even the robustness and colours of the clothes they select and by the leisure activities they choose. Even the mode of interaction may play its part, for fathers have been shown to play more physically with their sons – tossing them in the air, carrying them on their shoulders, teaching them, in fact, to 'be boys'.

From these examples and experiences, children by about age five or six, have developed a relatively enduring picture of 'what people like me do'. Those who don't conform are likely to have difficulty in forming friendships and those who can't may not benefit from taking actions which highlight their differences. In this research, several mums explained that they were uneasy because their sons were continuing to play alone, but were afraid that 'trying to get others to play' would make matters worse, because if this didn't work, it could highlight the children's difficulty even more. Much more research into knowing the best way to help friendships develop needs to be done.

CHAPTER 7

Developmental influences and changes in motor control

Most people associate the words 'developmental change' with the physical age-related changes which occur due to a basic biological process which is common to all. Implicit is the assumption that these changes will allow increased competence in all aspects of development, intellectual, social, emotional and motor.

To allow this to happen a complex interplay of factors – maturational, environmental, physical, intellectual and genetic – influence what can be done. This complexity explains why two children brought up in the same household can be 'chalk and cheese' and why bemused parents sometimes wonder, 'Where did I get that one?'

These factors need a brief explanation, always bearing in mind how they could affect children with movement learning difficulties.

Maturation

Gessell (1925) described maturation as 'genetically programmed sequential patterns of change', and for many years it was thought that these were independent of other influences. The physical growth pattern of children certainly seemed to show this. For in all children, maturation in physical development occurs from head to toe (cephalocaudal) and from the centre outwards (proximodistal). Cephalocaudal is the name given to the gradual progression of increased control over the muscle system and this, starting at the head, means that all children can hold their heads up before they sit, and sit unsupported before they stand. Children who have poor motor control over their lower limbs may have incomplete cephalocaudal development. Remember Ian and Derek, the children who had difficulty controlling their feet?

Proximodistal development refers to the control which begins at the centre of the body and moves to the extremities. As a result of this, young children can control their trunks and shoulders before their wrists and fingers, and teaching progressions, e.g. using a large, easier to hold paintbrush first, must mirror this developmental trait. Poor wrist and finger control may be due to incomplete proximodistal development. Ben, described on p. 20, had this difficulty. And as the large muscle groups develop before the small muscle groups, gross motor control generally develops first, fine motor control coming later.

An interesting concept is that of 'readiness'. An example which demonstrates this well is learning to walk. For children won't walk before they are ready, i.e. before they have the strength, balance and coordination to allow it to happen. Coaxing doesn't really help as the instructions for performing the basic movement patterns are passed on at the moment of conception. They are not taught.

If this is so, if the development of these patterns is preprogrammed, why should all children not achieve them at the same age and at the same level of competence? To find out we need to consider the impinging variables, i.e. heredity, environment, growth, experience and practice, in other words the nature (genetic) and the nurture (environmental) factors which cause developmental variation. This makes grouping children for teaching by chronological age questionable, to say the least!

Having said that, all countries produce developmental norms. These are compiled by finding at what age most children achieve different skills. Some of the 'youngest' tables describe motor patterns because these give some of the earliest, most visible signs of development. These biological clock patterns give a rough guide as to when children are progressing 'normally'. They also may cause parents unnecessary anguish if they do not realise that the 'normal' time span is wide.

Children with dyspraxia will reach their motor milestones towards the end of the 'usual time' although the patterns are likely to be of a poor standard (Ayres 1972).

Heredity

What is it that children inherit and how will this affect their motor competence?

Heredity has been described by Bee (1995) as a 'genetic blueprint which influences what can be done'. There is much debate about which factors are purely determined by our genes, but body size in terms of being slightly or heavily built appears to be one, although the influence of diet can't be ruled out. Height is another, but here there is regression to the mean – children of two tall parents may be shorter than either, for we do not keep on getting taller and taller! Height and body build can impact on what children are able or willing to do. Fragile youngsters are often reluctant to be involved in games which have contact for fear of being injured and heavily built children are not likely to choose activities which depend on speed or agility or changing direction quickly, or inversions where they must overcome their body weight. They fear embarrassment as well as incompetence.

Milestones of motor development from 2 to 6

Age	Locomotor skills	Non-locomotor skills	Manipulative skills
18–24 months	Runs (20 mo), walks well (24 mo); climbs stairs with both feet on each step	Pushes and pulls boxes or wheeled toys; unscrews lid on a jar	Shows clear hand preference; stacks 4 to 6 blocks; turns pages one at a time; picks things up without overbalancing
2–3 years	Runs easily; climbs up and down furniture unaided	Hauls and shoves big toys around obstacles	Picks up small objects (e.g. cheerios); throws small ball forward while standing
3–4 years	Walks upstairs one foot per step; skips on both feet; walks on tiptoe	Pedals and steers a tricycle; walks in any direction pulling a big toy	Catches large ball between out-stretched arms; cuts paper with scissors; holds pencil between thumb and first two fingers
4–5 years	Walks up and downstairs one foot per step; stands, runs and walks well on tiptoe		Strikes ball with bat; kicks and catches ball; threads beads but not needle; grasps pencil
5–6 years	Skips on alternative feet; walks a thin line; slides, swings		Plays ball games quite well; threads needle and sews stitches

Source: Connolly and Dalgleish 1989.

Figure 7.1 Developmental norms

Speed of movement is claimed as another inherited characteristic although if children have carers with a slow tempo as role models, it is hard to believe that this does not influence their own way of moving.

Parents are very often intrigued by the question of whether intelligence as measured by IQ is inherited. Studies of the IQ of identical twins reared together and apart normally provide evidence and make fascinating reading. Identical twins reared together have IQs that are highly similar – much more than fraternal twins (i.e. those that develop from a separate ovum, separately fertilised) reared in the same home. Environment does have an influence, however, as identical twins reared apart are less similar than those reared together. In studies of children adopted as babies, the children's IQ has been found to be much closer to that of the natural mothers than the adopted ones, a finding which strongly supports the genetic factor in IQ (Loehlin *et al.* 1994).

But even considering IQ as a 'pure' concept is problematic, because from the earliest days, the rapid developments in the brain benefit from, indeed require environmental support. 'Infants who grow in a complex environment develop more neural connections' (Bee 1998), and these allow a greater degree of learning to occur. If, as Trevarthen (1997) claims, 50 per cent of all learning happens in the first five years, the importance of children having a stimulating movement environment as well as an intellectual, social and emotional one, cannot be overestimated. Young children are skill hungry – and this certainly applies to motor skills. Whoever saw children walk sedately when they could run and skip and jump? They seek out movement challenges, e.g. jumping off a wall just for the sake of it, and if children actively seek out new experiences just for the sense of achievement they bring, they need appropriate feedback so that their progress is reinforced. This highlights the importance of sound teaching.

And so it can be seen that no characteristics are genetically 'fixed'. Children's behaviour is always a product of genetic and environmental factors. As an example of this interaction, children are born with certain response patterns, or inborn biases which stay with them throughout their lives and influence how they react to experiences and tackle new things. Almost without exception they choose to do the things they are good at and avoid those they feel they can't do. Once children realise that they have movement difficulties, avoidance is so understandable, but it means that they deny themselves practice and so the cycle of underachievement goes on. Teachers have to step in and provide appropriate movement learning programmes just as they would naturally do for reading or mathematics. Those who have tried and evaluated this kind of intervention by providing a daily movement programme, have been convinced that they have been successful in raising the children's confidence as well as their movement ability and furthermore that this has transferred to improving their attitude towards learning in other aspects of the curriculum. So intervention has a direct benefit and a most important 'spin-off', and the children gain on both counts.

According to Werner (1995), children are born with certain 'vulnerabilities', e.g. a difficult temperament, allergic reactions, or perhaps specific learning difficulties. But they also have some 'protective factors', e.g. a sunny nature, good coordination, or a good memory, and these help them deal with stress. The proportion of one kind in relation to the other determines whether children will be mainly resilient or vulnerable. These characteristics then interact with their environment and this explains why the children's perception of seemingly similar events may be quite different. Resilient children in a poor environment will fare better than the more vulnerable ones because they will make the most of their circumstances and seize any opportunities which the others miss. Vulnerable children really need parents who support them and help them become more confident. If this does not happen, and if they also have a poor environment, the outlook for them is extremely bleak, although amazingly, some do overcome appalling conditions and thrive.

Children with dyspraxia are going to be vulnerable in the area of movement development. They need extra encouragement and support so that they can progress and so that they can keep their difficulty in perspective, for although dyspraxia can be debilitating and frustrating and distressing it is not life-threatening.

Growth

Growth is another important factor, for most very young children long to be 'big'. At this early-years stage, growth proceeds at a much slower pace than during infancy. A steady height gain of 5 cm and weight gain of 2 kg each year is usual. Growth is different from maturation in that it provides a description of a physical process while maturation explains it. Heredity sets the limit on growth, but environmental factors determine whether it will be reached as children with a poor diet may not achieve their true height. In very poor countries, children's growth is likely to be stunted by malnutrition while in industrial, richer countries, dietary excesses, even obesity is more common. This tends to colour both the children's attitude to and participation in physical activity.

And of course 'potential height' can affect the kind of recreational activities which the children choose or those the parents choose for them. Perhaps they choose ballet for small-for-their-age girls and basketball for big-for-their-age boys or perhaps they look ahead to their children acquiring a high skill level – visualising Darcy Bussell or Michael Owen performances. While this is understandable, it might be better for their children to be in a group of active young children practising a wider range of skills.

Environment

Of course 'environment' is a much wider concept than the home environment although this is probably the most critical influence and certainly the source of early bonding and attachments which give the children long-lasting encouragement and support. The wider context will include facilities for learning and playing, friends of the same age nearby, schooling, the community and all the relationships and values and codes of practices therein.

For children with movement difficulties, Gallahue (1993) claims that the factors which play a crucial role in developing efficient and effective movement patterns are:

- opportunity to practise;
- facilities and equipment; and
- helpful and appropriate teaching.

He claims that failure to have abundant opportunities to practise and lack of encouragement prevents many children from gaining the perceptual and motor information they need to perform skilfully. Surely children who do not move easily are the ones who need opportunities to practise even more?

Another environmental influence which affects the possible provision of equipment and opportunities is whether one or both parents are employed. If both parents are out all day and come home very tired to face household tasks and children's homework, there may not be time or inclination to 'get active' and television and computer games may take over as the children's routine recreation, maybe even with crisps and coke!

Why is this not a good idea? After all, the children are safe at home, and they need to discuss programmes with their friends tomorrow; they aren't going to be 'sporty' anyway and they get PE at school, so is being active really worth the effort? Let's find out.

The benefits of movement

What benefits will children gain from being active? The statistics on children's fitness are frightening. The Shape of the Nation Survey (AAHPERD 1987) reveals that 40 per cent of children aged five to eight in America already have one coronary risk factor, i.e. obesity, high blood pressure, high cholesterol and/or low levels of physical activity. And while these figures have been questioned (Blair 1992), the Department of Health has taken them very seriously and made the promotion of 'physical activity and fitness' a top priority. It is convinced that activity is linked to good health and an associated sense of well-being.

Activity also promotes strength – activities such as running and bicycling helping leg strength, while lifting and swinging develop strength in the arms. Endurance is developed if the activities have a greater number of repetitions, e.g. aerobics.

Cardiovascular endurance concerns the heart, lungs and vascular system and is developed through exercise which is frequent and intensive. Swimming, running, cycling, if done with effort, are good choices. Mobility and flexibility are important benefits which can be gained if the activities encourage a greater range of movement through each joint. Unfortunately, although the PE programme in schools shows children the way things should be done, helps them to understand movement concepts and hopes to promote positive attitudes towards an active lifestyle, it does not have the curriculum space to make much change in fitness levels. This responsibility has to stay with the parents in the early years.

Having said all those things about the benefits, the dangers of an over-intense programme of exercise must be avoided because of possible soft tissue damage. It is very important too that supervision is by qualified people, not simply enthusiasts who, not understanding children's development, could unwittingly overstrain and damage the children in their care. Gallahue (1993) lists the following benefits of a regular programme of exercise:

Increased strength and endurance

- stimulates bone growth
- increases bone mineralisation
- reduces susceptibility to injury
- enhances self-concept
- enhances body-image.

Improved levels of cardiovascular capacity

- improves lung capacity
- strengthens the heart muscle
- improves circulation
- aids stress reduction.

Greater flexibility

- helps prevent injury
- increases work or play efficiency
- improves motor performance
- increases range of action
- promotes fluidity of movement (adapted from Gallahue 1993).

The main concern for those who are helping young children with movement difficulties, however, is to improve their performance in the basic movement patterns, because this will enable them to cope better with the activities of daily living and participate with a measure of competence in all the things their friends do.

Acquiring competence in the basic movement patterns

As children become better at moving, descriptors such as 'more precise', 'efficient', 'effective', 'energy-saving', 'rhythmic', and 'coordinated' can increasingly be applied. As this happens, the children progress from having an initial or immature pattern through an elementary stage until a mature pattern is achieved (see Figure 7.2). Some adolescents and adults will achieve a high-level sports skill performance, but generally only those with specific training would merit this claim. And so, in the early years it is important that teachers and nursery nurses understand the first three stages of development and are able to recognise them in action.

Progress will be steady for some children and erratic for those with difficulties. Nonetheless, over time the children's demonstration should move through the sequence towards the mature pattern end.

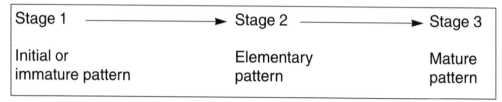

Figure 7.2 The stages of development of a basic movement pattern

Stage 1: initial or immature stage

At this early learning stage children's movements are clumsy and unrefined. The whole body takes part in the execution of the action rather than the necessary discrete parts and as a result there is a great deal of extraneous movement which hampers the pattern. Balance is poor and so the movement appears uncoordinated and arhythmic. When observing movement patterns at this stage, it is difficult to distinguish between the preparation, action and recovery phases. The whole thing happens in one haphazard burst of activity. Two or three year olds without difficulties typically function at this stage, but this continues longer if difficulties are present.

Stage 2: elementary stage

This is a transitional stage in which the children gain greater control over their movements. Increasing strength helps balance and coordination and the demonstrations become more rhythmical. Decisions about how fast, how much strength and where to move, however, can still be unreliable. Children at four or five typically move at this level.

Many adults have not gone beyond this stage in activities like throwing or in games like tennis which require manipulative skills, because they have not had or chosen to take the opportunity to have instruction or practice. Children with difficulties, even with practice, are likely to stay at this stage.

Stage 3: mature stage

At the mature stage, movements appear fluid and rhythmical. The preparation, action and recovery stages are well defined but integrated, so that the movement achieves its purpose efficiently. Control, balance and coordination are much better, but children's movements still lack the adult powers of strength and endurance. The mature stage in the basic movement activities can be achieved by most children at about six or seven. If children do not reach this stage, they will have great difficulty in acquiring sports skills at some later time, because these are embellishments of the basic patterns.

When observers assess the level of children's movement, they must remember that if the skill is new, then the learners will have to construct a mental plan of the activity and this will detract from the concentration given to moving well. And so the early tries are likely to be less successful than the eventual level of performance.

Answering question 5: 'How can we cope with assessing and recording when the children do all sorts of different movements?'

In this research, the teachers and nursery nurses explained that while their observational skills had 'really sharpened up and we are much more confident in making assessments now', and that was really good news, they were still perplexed by the enormity of their task. 'There are so many different kinds of movements', they explained. 'How can we cope?'

Categorising movement patterns

One way would be to categorise movements into three subdivisions, i.e. locomotor, non-locomotor and manipulative actions, as in Figure 7.3.

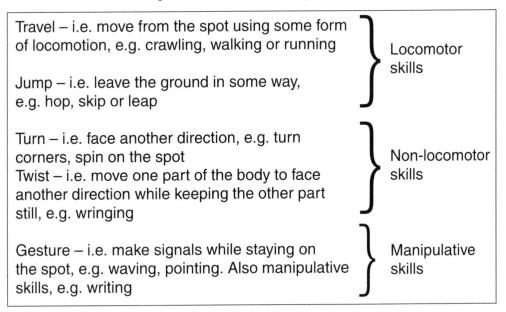

Travel – i.e. move from the spot using some form of locomotion, e.g. crawling, walking or running

Jump – i.e. leave the ground in some way, e.g. hop, skip or leap

} Locomotor skills

Turn – i.e. face another direction, e.g. turn corners, spin on the spot
Twist – i.e. move one part of the body to face another direction while keeping the other part still, e.g. wringing

} Non-locomotor skills

Gesture – i.e. make signals while staying on the spot, e.g. waving, pointing. Also manipulative skills, e.g. writing

} Manipulative skills

Figure 7.3 Categorising movement patterns

Observing movement and then allocating it to one of the subdivisions is a useful analytic tool because then reference can be made to the age-related patterns of development which give clues as to how children of different ages and developmental stages should be performing.

The variety in movement comes from the intention of the mover and any demands made by the environment, e.g. in obeying the rules of the game or coping with buffeting winds or rough paths. The following example will help to clarify.

The influence of intention

Picture children taking part in a number of activities. If one runs away from a friend in a game of tag, while another runs to kick a ball and a third runs into school, the basic action is obviously running, a form of travel, and a locomotor skill. The children's intention, however, changes the nature of the movement pattern.

In the first action, i.e. the game of tag, the intention is to run fast, probably in different directions to avoid being caught. The ground may be uneven making balance difficult and so holding the arms out may be helpful. The child will likely twist round as he or she runs to keep an eye on the chaser, and this top twist can throw the child off balance and affect the pathway. It will certainly slow the run by interrupting the rhythm of the running action. And the child may gesture 'keep away', or 'keys', laughing as he does so. The less nimble child is very likely to fall over!

The second child is running to kick a ball and the speed of the run is going to vary according to the position of any opponent. If it is a penalty kick, then the speed of the approach run can suit the kicker; the stress comes in placing the ball accurately into the net. If there is an opponent approaching, then the run must be fast, one eye must judge the oncoming pace and the body must prepare to swerve, or kick on the run to pass the ball. The running action has to be efficient and quickly adaptable before it can cope with these extra demands.

Running into school should be much less hazardous unless the child is late. But perhaps schoolbags have to be carried, and if the weight is over one shoulder, the young child is going to have to cope with a lop-sided action to compensate for the weight.

And so, in young children, the basic running pattern is rarely executed in its true athletic form. Nonetheless the basic pattern needs to be mastered before the game, the chase, the partner, the weight or the competition is added. Having children beat their own score gives an element of challenge without the competitive element which can work against good patterning. Certainly this strategy saves teams being chosen and the less able children being left till last, and if the equipment can be such that the children with movement difficulties have the larger bat or the airflow ball which doesn't travel quite so fast, then perhaps their scores can be gratifying too.

The basic movement patterns are shown in the following pages.

Travelling or locomotor patterns: walking, running, skipping and forward rolling

1. Walking

The onset of walking depends on maturation. Children usually walk between 12 and 18 months, some earlier. The mature walking pattern is typically achieved some time between ages 4 and 7.

Developmental sequence in walking

Initial or immature pattern	Elementary pattern	Mature pattern
1. Walking (a) Foot placed flat on the floor. Wide (sideways) base for balance	(a) Heel-toe pattern is established	(a) Smooth heel-toe pattern with effective propulsion
(b) Arms held out to assist balance	(b) Arms at side but not helping the movement	(b) Arms swing in opposition to legs to aid movement
(c) Whole body action swings leg round and forward	(c) Posture needs attention	(c) Well-poised action appears effortless
(No propulsion, balance is problematic)	(Slumping or tense shoulders can inhibit the action)	(Walking pattern alters to accommodate rough or uneven ground)

Look for and correct:

(a) poor posture;
(b) flat-footed action;
(c) toes turned out or in.

2. Running

Running is walking quickly with the addition of a flight phase during each step. Children show this flight or time unsupported by the ground at around two years. They can demonstrate this before they achieve the mature walking pattern. In the initial stages the same flat-footed action as in walking is evident, but gradually as balance and coordination improve, only a small area of the foot touches the ground.

Developmental sequence in running

Initial or immature pattern	Elementary pattern	Mature pattern
(a) There is no flight	(a) Limited flight phase	(a) Definite flight phase
(b) The body stays erect	(b) Slight lean forward	(b) Effective forward lean
(c) The support leg stays bent. There is little push off into extension	(c) Length of stride increases, as does speed	(c) Legs extend as they support weight, stride is long and regular
(d) The arms tend to swing out rather than forward/back	(d) Arms begin to help action by swinging forward/back	(d) Arms swing in opposition to the legs, punching forwards at right angles
(e) The base is wide for support	(e) Supporting leg extends to push body forward	(e) Speed is fast

Look for and correct:

(a) body twisting from side to side;
(b) arms swinging across trunk;
(c) landing on flat foot with no transference of weight forward;
(d) toes out or in, i.e. not in direction of action.

3. Skipping

A skipping action is a step-hop with alternate feet leading. The action should be continuous and rhythmical.

(Very often slowing the action and having the teacher and child or two children (one coping well) hold hands, so that the correct rhythm is passed from one to the other is helpful.) Some children, mostly boys, at ten can't skip!

Developmental sequence in skipping

Initial or immature pattern	Elementary pattern	Mature pattern
(a) Confusion in alternating foot pattern	(a) Step-hop pattern is coordinated	(a) Step is rhythmical
(b) Same foot leads the step-hop	(b) Pattern is rhythmical	(b) Pattern is efficient; no extra arm action or exaggerated lift of knees
(c) Arms either do not help the action or lift the body at the wrong time	(c) Arms help to lift the body but may cause the action to be over exaggerated	(c) Toe landing
(d) No basic rhythm	(d) Flat-footed step	(d) Change of direction happens without loss of pattern

Look for and correct:

(a) the same foot leading consecutive actions – a galloping step;
(b) the rhythm being uneven and the action jerky;
(c) the step-hop interspersed with a running action.

4. Forward roll

Rolling is a form of travelling as the body moves over the ground. The action can be performed for its own sake, that is as a discrete skill, it can form the transition between two other actions, or it can provide a means of safe landing from a height. Rolling allows the momentum of a fall to be absorbed safely into another movement which can help control. But because the momentum can pitch body weight forward, the rolling action must be instinctive and carefully executed. Hands must break the fall and transfer the body-weight on to the back of the shoulders then the hips so that standing is safely achieved! This is why rolling should be learned in a variety of ways, so that in falling from any direction, heads, elbows and shoulders tuck in and leave the 'padded bits' to take the weight!

Developmental sequence in rolling

Initial or immature pattern	Elementary pattern	Mature pattern
(a) Head does not tuck in but contacts mat	(a) Head still forward and tuck 'awkward'	(a) Back of head touches the mat lightly
(b) No momentum in pushing over from the legs, or from the arms	(b) Legs and arms still not helping to initiate or control the action	(b) Legs push off evenly and arms help control and balance
(c) Body flops or thumps over as the balance is on the head and the back does not round	(c) Action likely to fall to one side because of uneven push off	(c) Momentum returns body to standing position
	(d) Body begins action tightly curled then opens into an L position	(d) Control lasts through several consecutive rolls
	(e) Only one roll at a time possible	

Look for and correct:

(a) head coming down hard on to mat;
(b) feet not pushing with equal strength;
(c) arms failing to help balance and control;
(d) body untucking during action.

Flight patterns: jumping for distance and height

1. Jumping for distance: jumping/leaping from one foot to the other, or one foot to two feet

This action is similar to the run with the flight phase extended. Time in the air becomes important as the object of the exercise is to gain distance. Leaping requires greater amounts of strength and momentum to get the body into the air and balance during the flight is required to control the action.

Developmental sequence in jumping for distance

Initial or immature pattern	Elementary pattern	Mature pattern
(a) Confusion in knowing what to do	(a) Take-off foot is identified and used consistently	(a) Leg extends forcibly allowing take-off foot to drive forward
(b) No push-off from driving foot – no clear choice of preferred foot for take-off	(b) Action is still an extended run	(b) Body leans forward into the action
(c) Action is 'run' rather than leap	(c) Little flight – legs not extending from the push-off	(c) Momentum is used – arms and legs (in opposition) work together to help the action
(d) Arms are not used to help the action	(d) Arms used to help balance rather than to help the leaping action	(d) Rhythmical action
(e) Head comes 'down', body is tucked in the effort to leave the ground		(e) Body balance in the air
		(f) Controlled landing

Look for and correct:

(a) overlong run-up which confuses the action;
(b) a 'flustered' take-off, the child not making a clear decision as to which foot is the take-off foot;
(c) arms swinging widely and knocking the action off balance;
(d) head looking towards ground – bringing the body down before it goes up!

2. Jumping for height: vertical jump from one foot (or two) to land on two feet

This kind of jump may be taken from a 'still' position or it can follow a run. The direction is 'up' and the action requires a quick dynamic burst of strength. This necessitates a preparatory flexion of the body to gather strength and speed for the action.

Developmental sequence in jumping for height

Initial or immature pattern	Elementary pattern	Mature pattern
(a) No preparatory flexion	(a) Flexion excessive hampering action	(a) Flexion (60–90°) correct to initiate powerful action
(b) Poor extension of legs at take-off	(b) Legs do not provide power	(b) Forceful extension at hips, knees, ankles
(c) Head stays down	(c) Body does not extend in flight	(c) Action is coordinated into the lift and balanced in flight
(d) Arm action does not help to 'lift' the body – action is uncoordinated	(d) Arms help balance rather than lift	(d) Landing is controlled and close to take-off point
(e) Little flight		(e) Rhythmical action

Look for and correct:

(a) amount of flexion in preparatory crouch;
(b) arms not helping – watch timing of upward swing;
(c) poor extension – head keeping down;
(d) body overbalancing on landing.

Manipulative patterns: Throwing, Catching, Striking

1. Throwing (analysis – step, turn, swing, stretch)

In the early stages of learning to throw, the most difficult aspect is releasing the ball, which tends to drop at the thrower's feet. Gradually, as the elementary form is achieved, the difficulties are to do with accuracy and distance.

Developmental sequence in throwing

Initial or immature pattern	Elementary pattern	Mature pattern
(a) The action is led by the elbow which is held in front of the body	(a) The arms is swung up, side and back until the ball is held behind the head	(a) Throwing arms swings back in preparation – other arm is held in front to counterbalance
(b) The action is push from the elbow; the lever is short with little power	(b) Body turns towards the throwing side then bends forward with the arm action	(b) Body has wide rotation to the side in preparation
(c) The fingers are spread around the ball even at the moment of release	(c) Body weight goes forward over a wide base	(c) Throwing shoulder drops
(d) The body stays erect or leans back in reaction to the push	(d) Step forward with leg on same side as throwing arm	(d) Definite rotation through hips, legs, spine and shoulders during the throw
(e) Feet stay still		(e) Weight transfers from back to front foot – then back foot swings through to take weight in front
(f) The arm follow-through is forward and down		(f) Follow-through to fingers follows the direction of the ball

Look for and correct:

(a) throwing arm bent, elbow poking forward;
(b) no rotation of the body in preparation or in execution;
(c) inability to release the ball at the correct point;
(d) overbalancing due to arm swinging down.

2. Catching (analysis – reach, grasp, bend)

Catching is an absorbing moment which requires the child to make a number of estimations – e.g. the path of the ball, its pace and where a catching action will take place. Gradually the child learns to track a moving object in space and to move appropriately (i.e. in the correct direction at the correct speed) so that it may be caught. These are sophisticated judgements and plenty of practice with large balls is needed before the child can use small ones effectively. In skilled catching and throwing, the last phase of the catch action becomes the preparation for the throw.

Developmental sequence in catching

Initial or immature pattern	Elementary pattern	Mature pattern
(a) Child waits with arms outstretched (wide), hands apart, elbows at side	(a) Hands attempt to clasp ball, often miss and arms trap ball	(a) Hands swing to correct spot at correct time and grip ball deftly
(b) Body is erect, weight over the heels	(b) Timing is poor – due to undeveloped distance and pace judgements	(b) Arms give (to absorb force) on contact with ball
(c) The ball hits the body which bends to trap the ball	(c) Tension apparent in neck and shoulders	(c) The action is rhythmical and synchronised
(d) Fingers 'grab' at the ball rather than absorb and surround it	(d) Child does not always 'keep eyes on ball' for the entire trajectory	(d) Shoulders are relaxed
(e) Child may take avoidance action – shielding face with arms		(e) Eyes track ball into the hands

Look for and correct:

(a) stiff arms and hands;
(b) taking the eyes off the moving object;
(c) closing hands too early or too late;
(d) shutting eyes (avoidance action).

3. Striking

Striking is a propulsive movement which involves hitting an object towards a goal. The main categories are batting or kicking. For the first, the bat is used as an extension of the arm and when used firmly gives force and strength to the propulsion while in the second the foot is used to propel the ball. The accompanying body movement depends on the strength required to achieve the desired distance and how much time can elapse before the next striking action is required.

Developmental sequence for striking/batting/kicking

Initial or immature pattern	Elementary pattern	Mature pattern
(a) Bat/foot held in front of body – toe pokes at approaching ball	(a) Body turned to side in anticipation of oncoming ball	(a) Body rotates early
(b) Judgments of timing poor, i.e. distance and pace of oncoming ball	(b) Weight is transferred forward too early and so the hit lacks power	(b) Weight transfers from back to front foot
(c) Contact by luck	(c) Anticipatory or preparatory action delayed so action is rushed	(c) Correct amount of force applied at the correct time
(d) No trunk rotation or preparation back swing	(d) Contact is more secure but action lacks drive	(d) Action is smooth and rhythmical
(e) No follow-through after contact		

These movements patterns have been analysed by observing children and film sequences of children at different ages and stages. The work of R.L. Wickstrom and D.L. Gallahue has also been used extensively in providing these checklists.

CHAPTER 8

Activities to help

Answering question 6: 'What kind of activities will help alleviate the difficulties?'

Compiling an assessment profile is the first step towards helping children with problems, and the next is designing a programme to help the particular difficulties each child displays. Sugden and Henderson (1994) explain:

> Accurate assessment and successful management go hand in hand. Without a detailed assessment, an intervention programme cannot be geared to the individual needs of the child. Without a well formulated intervention programme, a detailed assessment is only of limited value.

But what kind of intervention programme? Digue and Kettles (1996) advise that one which can be done in short bursts of activity is the most productive strategy, as the children are only required to concentrate for a short spell and they don't become too tired.

It must be fun to do, and have in-built progressions so that the children themselves and their parents can see the benefits of their commitment and hard work. The activities need to be specially geared to the developmental progress which is required. Playing the piano will help rhythmic ability, flexibility in the fingers and fine motor coordination. This kind of exercise, however, does not offer a great deal of strengthening, apart from the small muscles being used continuously, because strengthening really requires some resistance, some kind of pushing or pulling or weight-bearing if it is to be effective, and activities must be designed to include this.

Moreover, the exercises should concern the specific competences which the children lack, for it cannot be assumed that transfer of learning from a general set of activities will directly help the underdeveloped skill. Strengthening exercises for the arms and fingers are just that; they don't directly make the children better writers. The increase in strength should give them better control over their pencils, but the skill of writing still has to be taught.

This is why Sugden and Henderson (1994) advise that 'The primary objective of all methods of intervention must be to improve the child's ability to function in everyday life.' And if the children are to cope each day with the multiplicity of tasks they will encounter, they need coping strategies. The most beneficial intervention, then, means balancing a programme so that teaching of specific movement skills which aid kinesthetic awareness, coordination, balance, rhythm and speed of movement, i.e. the movement abilities, leads on to showing the children, and hopefully their parents, how these relate to the acquisition of everyday coping skills.

As soon as pouring at the water tray is fairly reliable, then pouring juice at the snack table, i.e. helping with the activities of daily living, is one logical progression. As the children are enabled to make this kind of move, their teachers can gauge whether any transfer of learning has occurred or whether each specific skill needs to be taught in context.

Consistency is a key word in helping children with movement difficulties. If they know what will happen, i.e. the routine and that they will be able to do at least some of the activities well; if they know that the apparatus will not be frightening and that they will have a choice of activities; if they can be sure that expectations of the teachers will match their proficiency, then they can feel secure and be able to concentrate on moving as well as they can.

New movement additions should not be rushed. Instead of making the activities harder, encouraging the children to make up very short sequences of practised movements can give variety and a different kind of challenge. Once they understand the spatial concepts 'under', 'over' and 'through', as one example, they can try to organise some hoops, benches, canes and small apparatus for themselves, and build a sequence of linking movements. The other children can watch, calling out the directions as they do so, and thus the learning is reinforced for all. In addition, the teachers can see if the children can cope with sequencing and either add or take away items to match what they are able to do.

Given the difficulty some children have with copying movements, this other more creative kind of challenge can be appealing, and one which will help planning and organising as well as doing.

There are many activities interspersed throughout the text and in the following selection there are some to help children who enjoy routines, closed skills and metric rhythm, some to help develop imagination and others which allow the children to follow the rhythm which they themselves choose to impose upon the movements they try.

The following activities have suggested progressions and different choices can make up each programme. Before deciding on the composition, teachers need to decide what kind of exercises are required. If the aim is to develop flexibility then the range of movement in the joints must be increased, and if strengthening is the key, then exercises where some resistance is offered are necessary so that the muscles have to work hard. Alongside each activity in the following lists are the competences which will be helped. Do try.

Activities for early years children

1. Gross motor skills

Walking
Rope or coloured tape on the floor

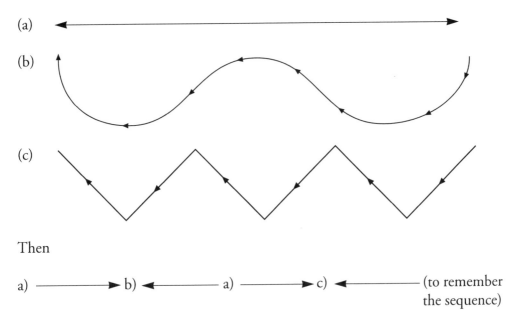

(a)

(b)

(c)

Then

a) ──────▶ b) ◀────── a) ──────▶ c) ◀────── (to remember the sequence)

HELPS

In a), encourage the children to walk carefully alongside the line, not necessarily on it, with a heel-toe action.

Body awareness

(b) and (c) are more challenging due to the gentle then acute changes of direction.
Encourage the children to move carefully and slowly, emphasising walking tall.

Propulsion

Good posture

Progression: Two children begin at different places and watch each other, aiming to finish at the same time.

Timing

Progression 2: Substitute crawling in (a). This is very important for coordination and vital if there is no climbing equipment.

Crawling

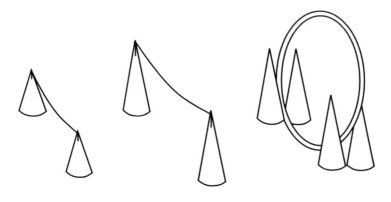

Jump over   Crawl **under**   Climb **through**

Add several hoops to crawl through.

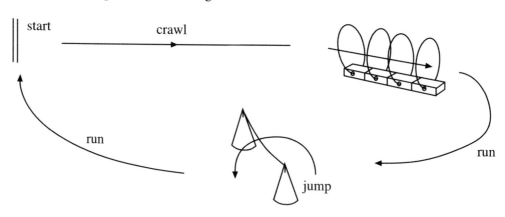

Children try not to touch the hoops.
Emphasise 'through', 'under' and then 'over'.

HELPS
Coordination,
directionality

Encourage children to call out directions as they move.

Conceptual understanding
of spatial terms

Progression: Children rearrange apparatus and remember spatial concepts.

Development of
ordering

Crawling and climbing
Crawl over a soft rolled up mat (carpet)
Crawl/climb up stairs (no hands as progression)
Jump down into a good space and run round to begin again

HELPS

Sequencing

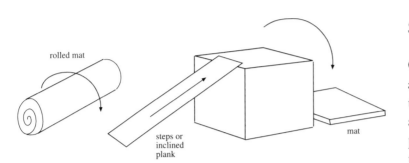

Climbing
actions using
the recovery to
aid the
preparation of
the next action

Progression:

Bunny jump over rolled carpet

HELPS
Strengthening
wrists (weight-
bearing)

This is a good visual sequence of activities.

Emphasise standing well – (pushing the back of the head
up) to begin and finish.

Marching and waiting
It is important that the following activities are done calmly and carefully with no
rush! 'Standing tall' gives an important sense of poise and body awareness.

HELPS
Rhythmical
awareness

For four and five year olds

March forward smartly for four steps and 'wait, wait, wait'   Control

March backwards for four steps and 'wait, wait, wait'   Listening skills

Repeat adding a clap on the wait

Teacher counts out rhythmically:

1 2 3 4 and wait, wait, wait
Back 2 3 4 and wait, wait, wait
Forward 2 3 4 and clap, clap, clap
Back 2 3 4 and clap, clap, clap

Body awareness
(marching tall,
heads high)
Rhythm
through
counting to 4
Awareness of
other children as
they keep in line

Progression:

(a)

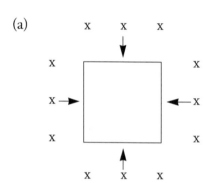

Children march
to edge of carpet
and back

Laterality
(awareness of
sidedness)

All children repeat the pattern they have already learned at the same time, perhaps substituting waving for clapping.

(b) Children on opposite sides go in and out at different times.   Judging size of
step

Jumping
(a) Feet together

Free jumping, feet together to build consecutive actions

Jump and jump and wait, jump and jump and wait.
Use arm swing to help propulsion forward.

Progression:

HELPS

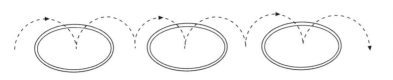

Coordination

Strong leg action

Continuous
movement

3 coloured hoops

Planning and
sequencing

Jump into hoops – 'Jump and jump and jump and out'; varying
distance.

(Some children will need to 'shuffle' to regain a good preparatory
position for the next jump, while others will 'jack-in-the-box'.)

One child per large hoop

Leg strength

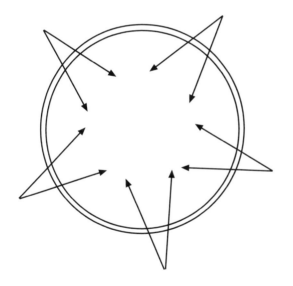

Control

Coordination

Rhythmic
development

Jumping in and out in all directions.

Teacher can accompany with tambourine. 1 and 2 and 3 and 4
(jumps).

Rest, get ready – now you're off. 1 and 2 and 3 and 4 and stand
quite still and tall.

Negotiating

Arrange bricks into paths

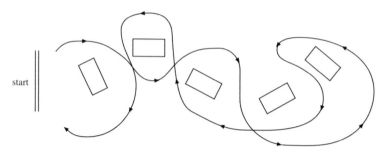

start

HELPS

Children have to stay just a whisper away but not touching, then run back. Children choose running, skipping, hopping, moving backwards.

Spatial awareness
Body boundary

Progression:

Bowl hoop or dribble football

Control and manipulation Skills

Hopping
Hopping over line (say six hops), RF (or preferred foot)

HELPS

Balance

Coordination

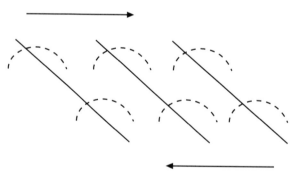

Body awareness
Partner awareness

And again using non-preferred foot.

Progression:

Two children approach at the same time, hopping four or six times
Bend down to touch other child's foot (hands on floor)
Regain standing
Change foot to hop back

Balancing

Walking along broad side of bench – head high, looking forward

Progression 1:

Hold hoop above head as you walk. Keep hoop steady!

Progression 2:

Walking along narrow ledge of bench, with light handhold where necessary. Then alone – trying to feel for position of next step rather than looking down.

Progression 3:

HELPS

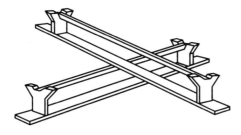

Balance
Coordination
Timing
Partner
cooperation

See-saw – two benches sit astride as see-saw
Teacher supervision required

Good poise
Body awareness
Leg strengthening

Progression 4:

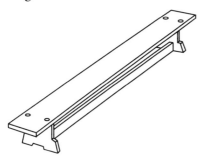

Balance
Segmented
movement
Body awareness

Single bench broad side up
One foot flat on broad side of bench. Push head high, come
   down to floor, push high, repeat.

Keep the same foot on the bench till the end.
Repeat using other foot on bench.

Progression 5:

Use the same activity but the narrow side of the bench. Offer   Coordination
some light support so that the child feels the extension.
Emphasise strong straight back and legs.

Progression 6:

Using either the broad or narrow side of the bench as
appropriate – Stand well, balance on one foot, arms
outstretched.

Draw as large a circle as possible with the other foot (allow time
between turns to correct any overbalancing).
Change over so that circling foot becomes balancing foot.

Bunny jumps

(1)   Freely on floor, emphasising weight evenly balanced on   Transfer of weight
      two hands looking forward and up.   from feet on to
                                                                     strong arms.
(2)   Over tape/rope or through hoop (trying not to touch   Weight-bearing
      hoop)   strengthening for
                                                                     arms/hands.

Progression for most agile children:

Child A holds hoop just above floor level.
Child B bunny jumps through, Child A moving hoop to clear feet.

Using action words

Running (tambourine; shake and shake and shake and HOLD)

Running in limited space, avoiding others – FREEZE   Negotiating

CRUMPLE down to the floor and SPRING up – (POP)   Listening for
                                                                    commands
and RUN –

| Progression: | | Rhythmical awareness |

Half the class stands still (making statues) while others weave in and out – after freeze all the children crumple, then spring up (POP). Change over. Partner runs. Emphasise direction, e.g. run forward, crumple down, spring up.

Partner awareness

(Leave enough time for children to cope. Use the action words, freeze, crumple, pop.)

Directionality

(For other ideas, see Appendix 3)

2. *Fine motor skills*

Equipment	Activity	Helps
1. Sand tray (a) Wet sand	Building castles, sand pies Pulling fingers through to make	Coordination (two hands) Finger awareness Strengthening and dexterity (continuous pathways)
(b) Dry sand	Pouring and filling Patting	Two-handed coordination Aiming: judging quantity Crossing the midline Hand dominance

2. Water tray
   + tubes and funnels
   + cake colours
   + ice
   + sponge
	Pouring and filling
	Syphoning
	Mixing
	Squeezing
		Holding implements at different heights for a longer time; spatial awareness
		Finger strengthening and dexterity

3. Clay	Moulding	Finger and arm strengthening

4. Scissors (+LH scissors) Paper (80–90 gsm) Stiff paper ⟶ light cardboard	Snipping fringes (rugs for doll's house or doilies for snack) then cutting between two straight lines, then easy curved patterns	Manipulation, finger dexterity: timing Two-handed coordination Hand–eye coordination
5. Beads – different colours All sizes – large and smaller holes Stiff string or tightly rolled paper cut in different sizes – previously painted by child	Threading – selecting sizes, colours, patterns	Two-handed and hand–eye coordination Sequencing (colours, sizes of beads) Completing a two-part task
6. Parachute	Billowing the parachute – one child running underneath to other side	Wrist strengthening Timing action in a non-competitive group
7. Lego Large bricks	Construction	Hand dominance Two-handed coordination Sorting and selecting Matching, balancing Crossing the midline
8. Table, cups, plastic knives etc.	Setting the table	Sorting, matching, one-to-one correlation
9. Shapes of coloured card. Small shapes held up by teacher, children run and stand on or by the matching shape on the ground	Teacher and small group in good space	Shape and colour recognition, tracking Problem solving
10. Hammer, wood, nails	Hammering	Two-handed/eye coordination Dexterity (pincer grip)

11. Dressing-up clothes – shoes and tutus, firemen's helmets, wedding dresses, kilts	Dressing and undressing	Dressing skills Ordering
12. Telephone with dial	Dialling	Finger dexterity Two-handed coordination Turn-taking
13. Computer	Keyboard skills Recognition of shapes, patterns	Tracking from screen to keyboard (vertical to horizontal) helping later copying from board Finger dexterity
14. Empty boxes	Imaginative play	Creative skills, partner play
15. Corners House, hospital, theatre, shop		Role-play activities of daily living Coping skills
16. Flour, water, margarine Baking, mixing, cutting, shaping, rolling dough	Teacher and small group	Two-handed coordination Pincer grip skills Hand strengthening
17. Finger puppets	In twos	Turn-taking Finger dexterity Role play

3. *Small games*

Game	Organisation	Helps
Simon says 'do this, do that'	Teacher and small group of children	Watching and copying Body awareness Response time Listening
Angels in the snow	Teacher and small group of children	Tactile awareness Spatial awareness
Head, shoulders, knees and toes Incy wincy spider and other singing games with actions	Teacher and small group of children	Body awareness Speed of movement Copying
In and out the dusty bluebells	Circle of children	Spatial awareness (under, through, round)
Party games e.g. musical beanbags (instead of chairs)	Teacher and small group of children	Listening and responding Speed of movement
Drama acting out well-known stories e.g. Jack chopping down the bean-stalk	Teacher and small group of children	Listening Swinging arms Rhythm development

Appendix 1 A movement observation record

Child's name .... Sex ☐   ☐

                                                                                  Male   Female

Age .... years .... months

This checklist is for one child who is causing you concern. Please record the child's usual level of competence rather than focusing on one unusual occurence. If, however the child's movement is erratic, making a general picture difficult or less than useful, please say that this is the case.

Before looking more specifically at motor development, please say whether you would consider that this was the child's only area of difficulty or whether there are other problems too.

Please tick if appropriate and add any other area of concern.

	Yes	No
Does the child have		
(a) Poor sight	☐	☐
(b) Low hearing	☐	☐
(c) A physical disability	☐	☐
(d) Difficulty in understanding instructions	☐	☐
(e) Speech difficulties	☐	☐
(f) Body-build problems	☐	☐
(i) very overweight	☐	☐
(ii) fragile	☐	☐
(iii) little strength	☐	☐
And is the child		
(g) Very tense and unsure	☐	☐
(h) Aggressive	☐	☐
(i) Lethargic – hard to interest	☐	☐
(j) Lacking persistence	☐	☐
(k) Seeking attention all the time	☐	☐

Any other difficulty? Please note below

The checklist now asks you to tick one box for each competence then give a mark out of ten for 'general coping ability' in that field. The boxes are 'Yes, can do it'; 'Some difficulty' meaning that the child needs real effort to cope; 'Severe difficulty' meaning that the child does not cope and 'Regression' which means that the child's performance is getting worse.

NB: This is a movement observation record to help teachers compile Assessment Profiles for school use or for gaining access to specialist help. It is not a test to determine dyspraxia.

Gross motor skills

Can the child	Yes, can do it	Some difficulty	Severe difficulty	Regression	Please give details
(a) Stand still, balanced and in control?					
(b) Sit still retaining poise?					
(c) Walk smoothly and with good poise?					
(d) Turn corners efficiently?					
(e) Walk on tip-toe with control (count of 6)?					
(f) Jump (two feet off floor)?					
(g) Kick a stationary ball?					
(h) Catch a large soft ball when thrown sympathetically?					
(i) Roll sideways and recover to stand with a good sense of timing and balance?					

Give a mark out of 10 for coordination in gross motor skills
Please give further details if appropriate.

Fine motor skills

Can the child	Yes, can do it	Some difficulty	Severe difficulty	Regression	Please give details
(a) Use a pencil/paint brush with control?					
(b) Pick up and replace objects efficiently?					
(c) Use two hands together to thread beads, build Lego or do jigsaws?					
(d) Draw a person with some detail of parts?					
(e) Dress in the correct order?					

Give a mark out of 10 for dexterity in fine motor skills ☐
Please give further details if appropriate.

Intellectual skills

Can the child

	Yes, can do it	Some difficulty	Severe difficulty	Regression	Please give details
(a) Talk readily to adults?					
Talk readily to children?					
(b) Articulate clearly?					
(c) Use a wide vocabulary?					
(d) Listen attentively?					
(e) Respond appropriately?					
(f) Follow a sequence of instructions?					
(g) Understand					
i. spatial concepts – over, under, through?					
ii. simple mathematical concepts – bigger, smaller?					

Give the child a mark out of 10 for intellectual competence
Please give further details if appropriate.

Social skills

Can the child	Yes, can do it	Some difficulty	Severe difficulty	Regression	Please give details
(a) Take turns with no fuss?					
(b) Interact easily with other children?					
(c) Take the lead in activities?					
(d) Participate in someone else's game?					

Give the child a mark out of 10 for social behaviour ☐

Emotional skills

	Usually	Sometimes	Rarely	Regression	Please give details
(a) Appear confident in following the daily routine?					
(b) Constantly seek attention?					
(c) Disturb other children?					
(d) Sustain eye contact?					
(e) Cope in new situations?					
(f) Appear aggressive or defiant?					

Give the child a mark out of 10 for emotional behaviour ☐

Please give further information at any point if you feel this would be appropriate. This could concern the areas already mentioned or different topics.

Thank you for completing this!

Appendix 2 Age-related development of movement patterns

	Locomotor patterns	Non-locomotor patterns	Manipulative skills
1 month		Can lift head from lying on front	Can retain object placed in hand
3–4 months		Stepping reflex pattern	Plays with hands as first toy
5 months	Rolls over from back	Holds head and shoulders erect when sitting	Stretching out to grasp objects
6–8 months		Sitting unsupported. Pulling up to stand	Reaching accurately. Grasping. Letting go
9 months	Crawling; climbing up stairs	Supports cup/bottle. Copes with finger food	Transfers objects from one hand to another
10 months	Walks around furniture	Bends to pick up object and stands again with one hand support	Makes toys work!
1 year	Walks unsteadily with feet apart and arms outstretched to balance	Will start games such as peek-a-boo	Plays with building bricks and others toys. Pulls off socks, shoes
2 years	Walks well, learning to run. Climbs on toys and furniture	Dismantles everything. Enjoys simple wooden lift out puzzles	Builds towers, pours water from one jug to another
2–3 years	Can ride tricycle. Climbs up and down stairs – both feet on each step. Walks on tiptoe	Enjoys jigsaws, painting, gluing	Can lift heavier objects with some control. Takes clothes off. Puts on pants, t-shirt
3–4 years	Learning to hop and balance	Can catch large ball Can release objects more easily now	Can draw circle. Buttons cardigan/coat
5 years	Can walk, run, skip and hop, even cycle and swim	Enjoys 'bunny jumps', and balancing activities	Can form letters and numbers. Hits ball with bat. Can tie shoes (5+)

Appendix 3 Action words chart

Actions	Words	Quality	Space	Combined actions
Travel	Dart, scamper, tip, plod, stride, rush, zoom, zip, dash, prowl, crawl, skip, hop, zig-zag etc.	WEIGHT Strong Light Heavy	LEVELS High Medium Low	Travelling/turning Darting/spinning Or Travelling/jumping Scamper/leaping
Turn	Swirl, twirl, wind, whirl, spin, whip, pivot, coil, pirouette etc.	TIME Quick Slow Sudden Sustained	DIRECTIONS Forward Backwards Diagonally Sideways	Turning/jumping Whirl/explode Turning/gesture Wind/sink
Jump	Leap, explode, fly, pounce, toss, shoot, pop, hop, bound etc.	SPACE Direct Indirect	PATHWAYS	Jumping/stillness Toss/freeze Jumping/travelling Bound/crawl
Gesture	Twist, gather, flop, crumple, stretch, surround, jab, slice, point etc	RHYTHM Metric Non-Metric	On the floor In the air	Gesture/jumping Crumple/pop Gesture/stillness Slice/hold
Stillness	Pause, hold, rest, wait, die, linger, freeze, sleep etc.			Stillness/travelling Linger/tip Stillness/jumping Wait/explode

Bibliography

AAHPERD (1987) *The Shape of the Nation: A Survey of State Physical Education Requirements.* Reston VA: NASPE.

Argyle, M. (1969) *Bodily Communication.* London: Methuen.

Ayres, J.A. (1972) *Sensory Integration and Learning Disorders.* Los Angeles: Western Psychological Services.

Bee, H. (1995) *The Developing Child*, 7th edn. New York: HarperCollins College Publishers.

Bee, H. (1998) *Lifespan Development.* London: Longman Publishers.

Blair, S.N. (1992) 'Are American children and youth fit? The need for better data', *Research Quarterly for Exercise and Sport* **63**(2).

Blythe, P. (1992) 'A physical approach to resolving learning difficulties'. Paper presented at the 4th European Conference of Neuro-developmental Delay in Children, Chester.

Bradley, L. (1990) 'Rhyming connections in learning to read and spell', in P.D. Pumfrey and C.D. Elliot (eds), *Children's Difficulties in Reading, Spelling and Writing.* London: Falmer.

Bretherton, I. (1991) 'Pouring new wine into old bottles: the social self as an internal working model', in M.P. Gorman, and L.A. Stroufe (eds), *Self Processes and Development.* The Minnesota Symposia on C.D. 57, 1151–65. 3.

British Child Health and Education Study (1985) 'Report to the Department of Health and Social Security,' in *Child Health.* University of Bristol.

Caan, W. (1998) Foreword, in M. Portwood, *Developmental Dyspraxia, Identification and Intervention: A Manual for Parents and Professionals*, 2nd edn. London: David Fulton Publishers.

Carlson, M. *et al.* (1988) 'The importance of regressive changes in the development of the nervous system: towards a neurological biological theory of child development', *Psychiatric Development* 7.

Chesson, R. *et al* (1990) *The Child with Motor/Learning Difficulties.* Royal Aberdeen Children's Hospital Aberdeen.

Child, D. (1986) *Psychology and the Teacher.* 4th edn. London: Holt Reinhart & Winston.

Connolly, K. and Dalgleish, M. (1989) 'Milestones of pre-school motor development', in H. Bee, *The Growing Child.* New York: Longman.

Cooley, C. (1962) *Human Nature and the Social Order.* New York: Charles Scribner.

Digue, A. and Kettles, G. (1996) 'Developmental dyspraxia: an overview', in G. Reid (ed.), *Dimensions of Dyslexia*, Vol. 2. Edinburgh: Moray House Institute.

Dishion, T.J. (1990) 'The family ecology of boys' peer relations in middle childhood', *Child Development* 61.

Dobie, S. (1996) 'Perceptual-motor and neuro-developmental dimensions', in G. Reid (ed.), *Dimensions of Dyslexia*, Vol. 2. Edinburgh: Moray House Institute.

Dussart, G. (1994) 'Identifying the clumsy child in school: an exploratory study', *British Journal of Special Education* 21(2).

Dyspraxia Trust (1991) *Praxis Makes Perfect.* Dyspraxia Trust: Hitchin, Herts.

French and Lee (1994) cited in Digue, A. and Kettles, G. (1976) 'Developmental dyspraxia: an overview', in G. Reid (ed.), *Dimensions of Dyslexia*, Vol. 2. Edinburgh: Moray House Institute.

Gallahue, D.L. (1993) *Developmental Physical Education for Today's Children.* Brown Communications: Dubuque.

Gessell, A. (1925) *The Mental Growth of the Preschool Child.* New York: Macmillan.

Gottman, J.M. (1986) 'The world of coordinated play', in J.M. Gottman and J.G. Parker (eds), *Conversations of Friends: Speculations on Affective Development.* Cambridge: Cambridge University Press.

Grimley, A. and McKinley, I. (1977) *The Clumsy Child.* Association of Pediatric Chartered Physiotherapists.

Gurney, P. (1987) 'Self-esteem enhancement in children: a review of research findings', *Educational Research* 29(2).

Harter, S. (1990) 'Processes underlying adolescent self-concept formation', in R. Montemayor, G.R. Adams and T.P. Gulotta (eds), *From Childhood to Adolescence: A Transitional Period?* Newbury Park CA: Sage.

Hartup, W.W. (1989) 'Peer relations in early and middle childhood', in B.V. Hasslet, and M. Hersen (eds), *Handbook of Social Development: A Lifespan Perspective.* New York: Plenum Press.

Kirby, A. (1999) 'What should we call children's coordination problems? developmental coordination disorder or dyspraxia?', *Dyslexia Review.*

Laban, R. (1942) *The Mastery of Movement*, 4th edn. London: McDonald & Evans.

Lehmkuyl, G. (1984) 'Ideomotor and ideatory apraxia in childhood', *Acta Paedopsychiatrica* **50**.

Loehlin, J.C. *et al.* (1994) 'Differential inheritance of mental abilities in the Texas adoption project', *Intelligence* **19**.

Maccoby, E.E. (1990) *Social Development: Psychological Growth and the Parent–Child Relationship.* New York: Harcourt Brace Jovanovich.

Macintyre, C. (1992) *Let's Find Why: An Introduction to Action Research for Teachers.* Edinburgh: Moray House Publications.

Macintyre, C. (1997) *Assessing Movement.* Dunfermline College Publications.

Macintyre, C. (1998) 'Helping children with movement difficulties', *Education 3–13: The Professional Journal for Primary Education* **26** (1).

McMillan, G. and Leslie, M. (1998) *The Early Intervention Handbook: Intervention in Literacy.* Edinburgh: City of Edinburgh Council.

Martin, C.L. (1991) 'The role of cognition in understanding gender effects', in H. W. Reese (ed.), *Advances in Child Development and Behaviour*, Vol. 23. San Diego, CA: Academic Press.

Offord, D.R. *et al.* (1991) 'The epidemiology of antisocial behaviour in childhood and adolescence', in D.J. Pepler and H. Rubink (eds), *The Development and Treatment of Childhood Aggression.* Hillsdale, NJ: Erlbaum.

Orton, S.J. (1937) *Reading, Writing and Speech Problems in Children.* New York: Norton.

Pope, M. (1988) 'Dyspraxia: a head teacher's perspective'. Hitchin: The Dyspraxia Trust.

Portwood, M. (1998) *Developmental Dyspraxia, Identification and Intervention: A Manual for Parents and Professionals*, 2nd edn. London: David Fulton Publishers.

Regehr, S. and Kaplan, B. (1988) 'Reading disability with motor problems may be an inherited sub-type', *Pediatrics* **82**(2).

Ripley, K. *et al.* (1997) *Dyspraxia: A Guide for Teachers and Parents.* London: David Fulton Publishers.

Rush, P. (1997) *Managing the Dyspraxic Child through Sensory Integration Therapy.* Conference presentation: Appleford School, Shrewton.

Russell, J. (1988) *Graded Activities for Children with Motor Difficulties.* Cambridge: Cambridge University Press.

Sherril, C. (1993) *Adapted Physical Activity, Recreation and Sport.* Cross disciplinary & Lifespan: Brown and Benchmark.

Singer, R.N. (1973) 'Motor learning as a function of age and sex', in G.L. Rarick, (ed), *Physical Activity, Human Growth and Development.* London: Academic Press.

Stephenson, I. and Fairgrieve, E. (1996) 'Dyslexia and the links with motor problems', in G. Reid (ed.), *Dimensions of Dyslexia*, Vol. 2. Edinburgh: Moray House Institute.

Stott, D.H. *et al. Test of Motor Impairment: Henderson revision.* Guelph, Ontario: Brook Educational Ltd.

Sugden D.A. and Keoch, J. (1991) *Problems in Movement Skill and Development.* University of S. California Press.

Sugden, D.A. and Henderson, S.E. (1994) 'Help with movement', *Special Children 75: Back to Basics 13.*

Trevarthen, C. (1997) *Play for Tomorrow.* Edinburgh: Video Production, Edinburgh University

Werner, E.E. (1995) 'Resilience in development', in *Current Directions in Psychological* Science 4.

Wickstrom, R.L. (1983) *Fundamental Motor Patterns.* Philadelphia: Lea & Febiger.

Witkin, H. A. and Goodenough, D. R. (1981) *Cognitive Styles: Essence and Origins.* New York International Universities Press.

Wood, D. (1992) *How Children Think and Learn.* Milton Keynes: Open University Press.

Index